ACHIEVING ADMISSION

How to Help Students Get into Selective Colleges and Keep Everyone Sane in the Process

David H. Nathan and
Nick J. Accrocco, EdD

Achieving Admission: How to Help Students Get into Selective Colleges and Keep Everyone Sane in the Process
By David H. Nathan and Nick J. Accrocco

Copyright © 2019 David H. Nathan and Nick J. Accrocco

ISBN-13: 978-1-7921-1486-1

www.achievingadmission.com

DEDICATION

For our parents, who put us through college,
our family, friends, and colleagues who helped inspire us,
and all the students we've worked with over years
who provided us with so many amazing stories and
memorable experiences,
especially Zach and Max, who made the whole process so
much more real.

CONTENTS

ACKNOWLEDGMENTS

Sincerest gratitude to Brooke Kushwaha for her hilarious and amazing artwork, Lydia Liu for her proofreading expertise, Aileen Zhang and Zach Nathan for their technical brilliance, Jamie Kim for her guidance, and Louise Ketz for her editorial assistance.

Thanks to our loyal focus group and editors: Sophie Caldwell, Iris Chen, Shani Israel, Sophia Kontos, Eli Maierson, and Pooja Salhotra.

Kudos to Clara Brotzen-Smith for her tireless work on the incredible book cover.

Much appreciation for the Gray Matters team of Lisa Gray and Allyn West, who provided us with a forum in the Houston Chronicle.

Special thanks to all those who showed demonstrated interest in the project, including Jeff Ritter, Adam Materasso, Pamela Penick, Marie Bigham, and Ed Graf.

COLLEGE ADMISSIONS AND THE UNEXPECTED VALUE OF IGNORANCE

PREFACE

THIS BOOK IS INTENTIONALLY DIFFERENT from the slew of college advice books out there. We wanted to create something that is not only entertaining and informative but also clearly explains what the college process is—and what it is not.

We offer some unique perspectives: David is a veteran English teacher who has helped many students with college essays while also having the loving (yet at times irrational) subjectivity of a parent. Nick has worked on both sides of the desk, in college admissions and counseling, with the caring (yet at times naïve) objectivity of *not* being a parent. Together, we know the joys and frustrations as well as the information and misinformation that can simultaneously illuminate and obscure the entire college application process.

There are some resources on the market that are all about finding ways to game the system to get into a top college. Other books promise you "proven" formulas and templates on how to write the perfect essay that will get you admitted to Harvard. (Have you ever noticed that all these books mention Harvard or the Ivy League by name but never any other schools or conferences? Why hasn't anyone published 25 *Essays Guaranteed to Get You into Duke or How to Crack the Pac-12?*)

We intend to give you the information you need to understand how admissions decisions are made and show what you can and cannot do to make yourself or your student more appealing to colleges.

We are both dedicated educators, not highly paid independent college consultants, and our hope is that we not only help you wrap your head around the often complex world of applying to college but that we also find opportunities to make you laugh along the way. The college admissions process *can* be fun, but you need an open mind. It also helps to acknowledge that applying to college is an important rite of passage for many high school seniors, but at the end of the day, students are filling out some documents to determine upon which beautiful campus they will pursue their higher education—it is hardly the Hunger Games.

We do not mean to diminish the sometimes shockingly raw emotions that the college application process can engender. Everyone needs to take a deep breath and realize that the hype surrounding the whole endeavor often dwarfs the reality. Sadly, more and more students (and their parents) are letting the hype affect them in some seriously harmful ways. We hope this book lends some insight, comfort, and humor to the process. We offer a mantra to our stressed students and panicked parents: *It will all be okay.*

Please Allow Me to Introduce Myself

Hello, I'm David. I became a high school English teacher before becoming a parent, and for 20 years (both in a large public high school and an exclusive college prep school) I helped get other people's kids into college. After decades of teaching students and writing recommendation letters and consulting on college applications, the time came for me to help my sons navigate the college process.

Going through the college search reaffirmed much of what I already knew, but it also revealed a seedy underbelly of strategic gamesmanship and an entire industry based on just *thinking* about where to apply. And then came the startling realization that *college could cost upwards of $50,000 more per year* than it cost me to attend back in the day.

In college, I had the good fortune of being a liberal arts major at a science and engineering school, so I wasn't subjected to the grueling pace and weed-out courses that many of my classmates endured. I eventually earned a double major in sociology and behavioral sciences (a hybrid of psychology, sociology, and anthropology), yet I didn't pursue a job in any of those fields.

Electives and extracurricular activities led to my eventual career path. Even though my school had no journalism department, I wrote for my college newspaper. Likewise, there was no theater major offered, but I became fully involved in acting, directing, and writing. And despite the absence of a School of Education, I took a few teaching classes and decided that it was a definite possibility down the road.

Throughout my career arc, I have written books, plays, short stories, screenplays, essays, and haikus. I have met professors that I still keep in touch with today. I even got to teach *One Flew Over the Cuckoo's Nest* to the grandson of my freshman English professor who first taught Ken Kesey's novel to me.

Years ago, when my first child was in middle school, he asked me what he should study in college. I told him—jokingly—that he could study anything he wanted, just so long as it had the word *engineering* in it.

Thirty years down the road, one of the constants I hear from people my age is that we remember far more about the college experience than we do about the specific classes we took. At seventeen, most students only have the faintest inkling of what they want to study, much less what they want to be.

As adults, we often think less of the kids today who are just as aimless as we once were.

If *Game of Thrones* offers any lesson in long-range scheming, it's that despite all the political maneuvering in the name of the children, it is important at the end of the day to keep one's head.

Hi, everybody! I'm Dr. Nick. As a college counselor, I have two main functions. First, I have to keep the office manager, registrar, and other support staff happy. If they are overwhelmed and frazzled, the whole department falls apart fast—but that's another book, and I doubt you opened up this one to learn about office management.

My other task is, simply, to calm students and parents down.

For a long time, I really had no clue what I wanted to do with my life. I initially hated history and the humanities in high school (that is not to say I was any sort of budding scientist or mathematician either). I had a few teachers who really kicked my butt, which eventually spawned a true lifelong love of history and people. Thus, to my father's horror, I entered college as a presumptive anthropology major with a history minor, only later to become a double major in both with a European studies minor.

When I worked as an undergraduate tour guide for prospective students, I would tell families about my hometown, proclaim I was a student in the College of Arts & Science, and then I would rattle off my majors. Inevitably, a parent (clearly freaking out that their impressionable child might follow in my footsteps) would ask with a high degree of passive aggression, "What are you going to do with that major?"

At first, I didn't have an answer prepared, not even a glib one. For a while I would address these derisive queries by talking about the value of a liberal arts education (which I still firmly believe). Eventually I just started half-heartedly replying that I would "go into law," which would usually satisfy the parents so we could resume the tour. While I would eventually study education in graduate school, I am quite grateful for my undergraduate disciplines: they taught me how to think.

Over the years, I have met countless students who are brilliant in their chosen field or path, and I am in awe of their talent. While I can't do what they can do, I can help them get to a place where they can succeed. That's what this book is all about.

Parents Just Don't Understand

Families face a college admissions conundrum: The kids have never been to college, so the whole experience is new and thrilling yet terrifying, and those parents who have been to college have not gone through the undergraduate application process in two or three decades. There are also families in which neither parent has gone to college, and they face an entirely different array of challenges. A lot has changed over the years, mom and dad, but don't worry—we will get you caught up.

Kids, just a reminder: If and when your parents applied to college, they used rotary phones (and they might have gotten a busy signal), they went to arcades to play video games, college applications were filled out by hand or on a typewriter (usually at mom or dad's office), and lots of seniors applied to schools without ever making even one college visit!

If you are reading this book, you are either trying to get into college or you have a vested interest in getting someone into college—and not just any college, but especially a "Highly Selective" College (what we prefer to call **The Ultras**). Luckily, you are our target audience.

Pro Tips and More

Throughout the book, we will share with you some **SUBURBAN LEGENDS** that will hopefully dispel some of the corrosive misconceptions making the rounds, like the story of a friend of a friend who heard that her niece's neighbor got a perfect SAT score and was still rejected by her safety school. We will also drop in lots of **PRO TIPS**, **FUN FACTS**, and **GET REAL** features to help you keep everything in perspective

And here is your first one:

GET REAL: If you feel, deep in your core, that you or your child deserves to attend a prestigious school, then you should remember the sage words of Old West outlaw Bill Munny in *Unforgiven*: "Deserve's got nothing to do with it."

R-E-L-A-X

It is unsurprising that in this highly competitive (some say "toxic") atmosphere that surrounds the college admissions process, people are looking to game the system without really knowing what they are doing—or why.

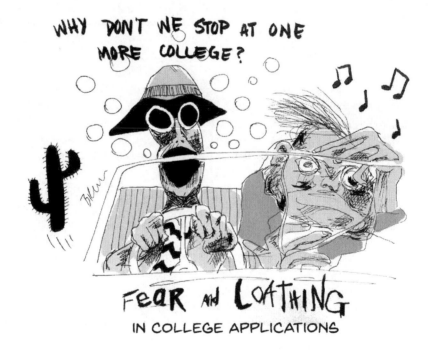

Our purpose in writing *Achieving Admission* is to dial back the crazy and provide some reasons to Keep Calm and Apply On (or just like Green Bay Packers quarterback Aaron Rodgers counseled fans in 2014 after the team got off to a slow start: "Relax").

Yes, college acceptance rates at some of the most selective colleges are now well under ten percent (Panic!). On the other hand, there are perfectly happy people who attend hundreds of fantastic colleges and become hugely successful (Chill Out!).

Recently, a family came in to visit with Nick, and during the meeting they asked if he liked their child's essay. Nick assured them that he indeed liked the essay. Then the student looked at Nick and asked, "But do you *really* like it?" Then it was the mother's turn to question if her son's work was good enough. Finally Nick said to everyone, "You're not listening because you're looking for something to worry about."

Sometimes it is as simple as that—we worry because if we remained calm about the future, we would not know what to do with ourselves.

If Gonzo journalist Hunter S. Thompson were around today, he might have written *Fear and Loathing in College Applications*, but he did once offer a solid piece of advice that can be applied to hopeful applicants: You bought the ticket, take the ride.

A Note on Writing This Book or: The Man with Two Brains

Even though this book is the collaboration of two people, from here on out we will be writing mostly in first-person singular. You might surmise that any of the anecdotes about having a child applying to college will be from David's perspective, and the stories about working in college admissions will come from Nick. There is, however, significant overlap in our experience visiting colleges, working with high school students, assisting with applications, and knowing the most reliable and current admission information. And when we share anecdotes from our youth, you will just have to figure out which one of us is writing.

We (I) hope this isn't too confusing.

50 SHADES OF ADMISSIONS

CHAPTER 1

Everybody needs a change, a chance to check out the new. But you're the only one to see the changes you take yourself through.

— Stevie Wonder, "Don't You Worry 'Bout a Thing"

W HENEVER I GO TO A HARDWARE STORE, I often look at the samples of paint colors. Not because I have ever painted a wall (or much of anything for that matter), but I just marvel at the names of the colors. I do not understand how certain colors get their names.

Years ago, when it came time to choose a new color for the college counseling office, my colleagues picked a beige-pinkish color called—I kid you not—Puppy Paws. [Note: Most guys only know the names of colors in a 16-count box of Crayons. Any other color is just a combination of those basic hues.]

I also do not understand why I am so enamored with color names, but I always thought it would be a fascinating job. I wonder how one goes about getting a job naming paint colors. What would be the qualifications? An art degree? Superior writing skills? Improv comedy?

In 2017, research scientist Janelle Shane even tried to program a neural network to invent new paint color names—with hilarious results—including such head-scratchers as Stoomy Brown, Bank Butt, and Light of Blast.

If there was a paint color called College Admissions, it would definitely be a shade of gray. (Feel free to insert your own *50 Shades of Grey* joke here—the parallel between applying to college and a relationship filled with S&M is too good to pass up).

College Admissions Gray would be the perfect balance between Cool Whip White and Outer Space Black. (See? I can totally name colors!) But does College Admissions Gray look good in a room with an Ivy exterior? The answer: It depends.

FUN FACT: Nick actually had his College Counseling department walls painted gray during the writing of this book.

The Universal Disclaimer: It Depends

"It depends" is the answer to almost any question anyone has ever had or will have about college admissions. It is as maddeningly vague as it is precisely accurate. And that is why everyone has heard rumors and myths—all with grains of truth sprinkled over large fields that are fertilized by a proprietary blend of manure made from a mixture of misunderstanding, hyperbole, and nonsense. It is why students and parents and teachers and counselors are stressed out. And it's probably why you are reading this book.

The reason why this disclaimer is so important to remember is due to the diversity of educational institutions and their often similar—yet sometimes divergent—**institutional goals**.

GET REAL: The reason any student is admitted to an institution is because one or multiple factors about them are meeting institutional goals, which is what the admissions process is trying to achieve. In other words, the "really, really sweet" student everyone loves (including the admissions office) with an application that does not meet any institutional goals is less likely to be admitted.

Institutional goals, like the institutions that seek to achieve them, can vary. Broadly put, they are as follows: strong academics, high test scores, high class rank, equal gender breakdown, diversity (e.g., ethnicity, religion, socioeconomic status, and cultural background), international students, talented athletes, artists (performing or studio), geographic representation, development cases (i.e., large donors), and influential people whom the college needs to keep happy.

The preceding list is full of hot-button, controversial issues that many students, families, and educators embrace, bemoan, decry, or question—and all with good reason. You may find yourself wanting to know the ins and outs of each and every one of the aforementioned categories. Never fear, there is plenty of detailed discussion throughout the book, but for now, remember the answer to every question about the college admissions process: *It depends.* The institutional goals are common criteria, but they are not found at every institution, and they are certainly not weighted equally when it comes to admissions.

Most colleges want strong academics, but what if they are "open-enrollment"? A growing number of colleges are making the submission of standardized test scores optional; in 2018, the University of Chicago announced that they would no longer require SAT or ACT scores. Other notable schools that are test-optional include Wake Forest, George Washington University, Brandeis, Worcester Polytech, and Bowdoin.

PRO TIP: This one is surprisingly simple—you can always just call the admissions office and ask them how a particular factor is considered within the selection process.

An Unequal Playing Field

Some students do not attend a high school that computes and publicizes exact class rank, and admissions offices cannot make class rank a factor if it does not exist. A student's ethnic and personal background will often be considered when evaluating an application, but schools like the California Institute of Technology (Caltech), do not consider these factors.

For some colleges, athletic and artistic programs are of great concern, yet possessing these talents may be a minor consideration at another university.

Public state institutions favor students from their home state, and they often cost far less for in-state students.

And, yes, some students will be admitted because their family is well-connected with the administration and/or because they are super-wealthy benefactors of the college, but many of these students could be admissible on their own merits—after all, **family income is the most reliable predictor of standardized test scores.** Just because someone is rich does not mean they cannot also be one of the best and brightest. For all the wailing and gnashing of teeth, the actual number of students using connections and wealth as an entrée to admission is actually quite small.

Consider institutions such as Berea College in Kentucky. Their mission is to educate underserved students who are usually the first person in their family to attend college and who come primarily from the Appalachian mountain region—and they charge no tuition. Spend just a little time away from U.S. News & World Report (everyone's favorite whipping boy—*unless it makes their college look good)*, and you can see the vast array of colleges and the many overlapping and totally discrete institutional goals that colleges have.

That's why the answer to many frequently asked questions is *it depends*. That's why students and parents are often confused and anxious. And that's why every college counselor should not paint their accent wall with Puppy Paws but instead with College Admissions Gray.

THE ANTHROPOLOGY OF ADMISSIONS

CHAPTER 2

Well we know where we're going,
but we don't know where we've been.
And we know what we're knowing,
but we can't say what we've seen.
And we're not little children, and we know what we want.
And the future is certain, give us time to work it out.

— *Talking Heads, "Road to Nowhere"*

WHILE WORKING IN ADMISSIONS at Vanderbilt, I once heard a dean of admissions say in regard to the college search process: "We deal with people's children and their money—it doesn't get much more personal than that."

And it is personal. Deeply.

Not only does money provide the means to sustain life and acquire what one wants and needs, but it can also be used to garner a stronger social status.

One of my favorite 20th-century thinkers is French sociologist-anthropologist-philosopher Pierre Bourdieu. Some of his most famous work revolves around the idea of different types of **capital** and how one form can be exchanged for another. **Economic capital** refers primarily to money, and Bourdieu explains how it can be used to obtain other forms of capital: **symbolic** (honor, prestige), **cultural** (academic knowledge, personal skills), or **social** (who you know in society).

If we consider the tuition paid by families, or even the need-based financial aid and scholarships provided by institutions of higher education and nonprofits, then we can view the symbolic, cultural, and social forms of capital at work during the college search. Within the college admissions process, Bourdieu's theories and framework are profound.

Striving for a Fairness We Never Quite Obtain

The higher the socio-economic status of a student's family, the more capital (of all forms) they are likely to possess. **The college admissions profession, which truly strives for a meritocracy and fairness far more often than not, must contend with the reality that students are not (and cannot begin) on an even playing field.** The finish line is closer, and overall choices for higher education are more plentiful, for those with larger pools of economic, symbolic, cultural, and social capital.

Some students have significant advantages over their peers in the college process by receiving individual test preparation and college application assistance, attending an academically prestigious high school, and knowing how the admissions process works or even (in extreme and, perhaps, overly reported cases) knowing an influential person at the institution.

Of course, these advantages are imparted to students by their parents, whose accumulation of the various forms of capital will have significant and profound effects (not to mention the expectations of where their child will be admitted) that will determine much of the path toward college.

While college admissions offices are well aware of the vast differences in economics and resources within school communities and take care to consider those differences, it can be a daunting task when you think about the diversity of high school communities and the need to meet institutional goals. As a former Vanderbilt dean of admissions used to say, "We strive for a fairness we never quite obtain."

Speaking of Unfair...

On March 12, 2019, the final edits were being made on this book. And then all hell broke loose.

Federal prosecutors had just announced the largest college admissions scandal ever prosecuted. Fifty defendants, including 33 parents, nine college coaches, two SAT/ACT test administrators, and an SAT exam proctor were charged with bribery and cheating on standardized tests. The sheer audacity of the operation, which brought in $25 million over eight years and involved over 750 students, sparked universal outrage and seemed to confirm everyone's worst fears that, when it comes to getting into highly selective colleges, there are no limits to what people will do.

One of my former students even suggested that we should change the title of the book to *Achieving Admission: Without Spending Millions on Bribes*

So let's get this straight before we go any further, we wrote this book to help parents and students understand the college admission process better. It is not intended to help students sneak in the back door or enter illegally through the "side door" as ringleader William "Rick" Singer referred to his method of bribery and faking student credentials.

Parents, it should go without saying that it is never acceptable to have your child fraudulently diagnosed with a learning disability so they can receive extra time and then fly them to Los Angeles so a corrupt SAT/ACT administrator can help them raise their score hundreds of points. Do not pay thousands (or millions) of dollars to shady test prep gurus who will then bribe coaches to accept your kid as an athlete even though they don't actually play the sport. Do not hire anyone to take the SAT or ACT in your child's name or come in after they have taken the test and change the answers. Do not send the message that your child is unable to get into college unless you pull strings, hire someone to write their college essays, or do anything else that would reduce the pride they will feel when they get into college on their own merits.

Students, take responsibility for your educational future. Be patient with your parents throughout the process—but not if they pay $6.5 million to bribe people so you can take the place of a more qualified applicant. Do not feign ignorance if your SAT score miraculously goes up 400 points after your parents fly you across the country to take the test. Even though your parents might be corporate CEO's or famous actresses, you still have do the work necessary to earn your place in the freshman class. If you are aware that your parents have paid to get you in the side door, realize that when they get caught or you get found out, you may very well get kicked out of school or have your diploma rescinded.

End of sermon.

The Needs of the Many Don't Outweigh the Needs of the Few (Or the One)

Most parents do not concern themselves with the big picture. In fact, a hard lesson I learned as a high school college counselor was that the vast majority of parents couldn't care less about the larger trends or education policy implications for future classes and students.

All the stuff I cannot get enough of—because, like most folks in college admissions and counseling, I am a proud, unashamed educational practitioner and geek—is of absolutely no interest to harried parents just trying to get their child into college.

Try as I might to explain the process and describe how the proverbial sausage is made, many parents respond quite brusquely, often with contemptuous disinterest as they bemoan the perceived unfairness of the process because their child was not getting what they deserved (Translation: deserved = wanted).

One of my earliest experiences at Vanderbilt was when I was doing the best I could to explain to an upset mother why we had waitlisted her very likeable and totally admissible daughter. I attempted to thoroughly clarify the imperfect admissions process to her, but she continued to unload her frustration on me. Hell truly hath no fury like a woman whose daughter has been waitlisted.

Back then I shared an office with a veteran admissions colleague (also a mother of two) who overheard our conversation. When my phone call with the irate mother ended, she said, "I can see your heart is in the right place, and you tried to explain to her the competitiveness of the situation, but she just wants to be heard and vent. Next time, just listen and keep saying, *I know! I know!*"

Years later, working on the high school side, I was explaining to a distraught father how a change in state law would benefit future applicants. "I don't care about that," he replied. "I just care about *my* son."

Lest you think I am suggesting that these parents were out of line, nothing could be further from the truth. After all, it's their kid. In the 2013 romantic comedy *Admission*, Tina Fey plays a Princeton admissions officer who acknowledges that one of the toughest parts of the job is dealing with "parents who just realized there isn't room for every organically fed, well-tutored offspring."

I have worked with many students over the course of my career, and I have stayed in touch with some of those students for years, wherever life takes them, long after our work together has passed. Plenty of them have been joys to work with, and there are those (naturally) that I cannot wait to see graduate. I care about each and every one of them and their success in education and life—regardless of academic ability, athletic or artistic prowess, or intended field of study. That's because I'm a counselor, and that's what I do.

Here in Status Symbol Land

There are powerful social forces at play when it comes to the college application process. In simple anthropological terms, there are two types of status: achieved and ascribed.

Achieved status is acquired by doing something: Winning a tennis tournament, making the Honor Roll, or getting into Amherst.

Ascribed status is the result of being born into a particular family or gender. As we will see, getting into college can, to some extent, be considered a result of ascribed status. Yes, students must achieve their admittance to a college, but a good deal of what determines college readiness is determined by birth.

In an effort to achieve college admission, students try to accumulate as many impressive accolades as they can, but it is up to the colleges to determine how many of those accomplishments meet their institutional goals.

Know Your Players

Let's think about the four key players in a student's college search: **dean of admissions, admissions officer, college counselor,** and **parent.** These four adults are all responsible for key components along the way to determining which college shirt seniors will be wearing on T-shirt Day.

The dean has the most institutional knowledge about what a college is hoping to achieve, yet this person probably does not have much emotion invested in any single applicant because deans are looking at the entire pool of applicants.

The admissions officer has a strong degree of institutional knowledge but is not likely to be sitting in on any upper-level administrative meetings, and (contrary to the popular belief) they will want to advocate in favor of admission for their applicants. They travel their territory, they meet the students, and they work with the high school counselors. **Admitting students to college is much more fun than denying them,** yet I was often surprised by how many parents would call me when their son or daughter was waitlisted and tell me that I had "ruined their child's life." What they didn't realize was that I very well may have argued for upwards of an hour in committee for their child's admission.

The nature of the highly selective institutions where I worked was partially what got me interested in moving to the high school side. I got tired of denying great students every year. All these denials were not due to some nefarious proclamation from the administration. We simply had far more students applying than spots available.

Today, as a former admissions officer who has become a **college counselor** (or **guidance counselor** if you prefer), my knowledge of the admissions process stems from experience and staying current through professional development workshops, conferences, and good old-fashioned networking. The admissions process does not change all that much from year to year, and most of those changes are minor and widely disseminated by the colleges.

One of the reasons I switched to the high school side is because I knew that I could assist students far more effectively if I were helping them understand the admissions process.

The applicants I worked with as a college admissions officer were typically high school students I might meet once or twice during the recruitment process and who were later represented by a folder full of papers. But as a high school counselor, these applicants became people I saw every day on campus: I greeted them in the hallways, I watched them during assemblies, I cheered for them on the athletic fields, and I calmed them down when they burst into my office in a panic.

Warning: Parental Advisory

If you are a **parent**, you likely have no idea exactly what the colleges are looking for, but you keep getting bombarded by the media, relatives, and other parents about what you should know. You've no doubt heard of the most prestigious schools (the ones famous for being famous) and the highly respectable institutions within your region, but there are hundreds of fantastic colleges and universities out there. How can you possibly know enough to be of assistance in the college process?

If you live in Texas, you may very well extol the virtues of some colleges in your region like Rice, Trinity, or SMU, but then you might scoff at other highly regarded schools such as Rensselaer Polytechnic Institute, Sarah Lawrence, or Colgate in upstate New York. And all those New Englanders might sing the praises of Williams, Wesleyan, and Boston University, but they might not even consider schools North Carolinians love such as Davidson, Elon, and High Point University.

Chances are astronomically high that parents have zero admissions or financial aid experience. With all due respect to the parents of children who have already gotten into college: No, having an older child go through the process does not make you an admissions expert any more than taking your child to have a cavity filled makes you a dentist or graduating from high school 30 years ago makes you qualified to be a teacher (or any more than going in for a rectal exam makes you a proctologist—but the prognosis is probably the same—you are likely full of it).

What you need to keep in mind when chatting with friends who claim to have "gotten a child into a top college" is that *they don't really know how it all works.* There is no one-size-fits-all method for gaining admission to highly selective schools.

A parent is in the absolute reverse position of the dean of admissions. Not only do they know close to nothing, but it's *their* child. Inevitably, parents will highlight their son's and daughter's accolades with great pomp while simultaneously downplaying any shortcomings (real or perceived) with their child's admissions competitiveness. I cannot blame them, and who could? We love our children and want what's best for them.

The problem is that many parents cling to several misconceptions of how "best" is defined. I have yet to hear a parent tell me anything other than "I want my child to attend a good college." It is hard to imagine a parent saying they want their kid to attend Subpar University.

These parents cling to dubious notions of academic quality, including perceived prestige fueled by any sort of rankings (all of which result in different outcomes based on flawed methodology). A low admit rate and brand name recognition are also key for some parents. They understandably subscribe to this herd mentality because the pressure on them is as enormous as it is deafening, which unfortunately limits the options for their child to have a happy, successful college life. I feel for these parents, and I wish more understood how much I care and that I *do* know the college search process *and* have their child's best interest at heart.

Prepare Your Child for the Path, Not the Path for Your Child

Much has been made of parental involvement over the past decade. There are **Tiger Moms** who stop at nothing to drive their children to greatness or **Helicopter Parents** who hover over their kids to make sure everything gets done.

Parents who have been educational partners (or enablers, depending on your perspective) to ensure that their children excel—all in the name of college—will undoubtedly be intimately involved in the college application process: taking kids on college tours, reading all the college brochures that their kids ignore, and asking all the questions on college tours because their kids won't say a word.

Lately, overly involved parents have been morphing into **Lawnmower Parents** (also dubbed **Snowplow Parents**). These are often well-meaning parents who attempt to clear away all obstacles for their kids. The downside is that despite all the perceived advantages they are bestowing on their children (like obsessively checking student grades and assignments online), these parents are sapping their students of the self-confidence and backbone needed to survive when they move away from home.

Even Bart and Lisa Simpson needed to let their father know when he was trying too hard to be a good parent:

> **BART**
> No offense, Homer, but your half-assed under-parenting
> was a lot more fun than your half-assed over-parenting.
> **HOMER**
> But I'm using my whole ass.

The result is a generation of kids known as **Teacup Children**: oh-so-pretty, but oh-so-delicate—and they crack easily.

Recent studies, including a 2015 article in the New York Times ("Suicide on Campus and the Pressure of Perfection"), describe the plight of many students who feel the weight of high expectations but do not have the life skills with which to handle these expectations.

Parents play the college admissions game at their own peril—those who make getting into the "right" college the sole priority for their children may deprive them of any sense of normalcy.

A colleague of mine once said in passing that she had heard about one family that planned on taking an entire year off from work in order to research colleges. I even once had a parent take her daughter on over 30 college visits—and they didn't like any of them!

Ironically, the methods that parents utilize to ensure that their kids get into college may very well be the reason that these students are so ill-equipped to excel once they arrive on campus.

PRO TIP: When parents talk about their child's college search process, they should avoid using the pronoun "we." After all, *we* are not applying to college—your kid is.

We Want What's Best* for Our Kids (*If U.S. News & World Report Says It's Best)

I am a self-professed college admissions nerd. I have always found the process strangely fascinating, most likely because working in college admissions is an intriguing way to learn about society. You get to see so many different types of students, families, and school communities. The travel on either side of the desk takes one all over the country and beyond.

There is something distinctly American about the access to higher education. Americans champion equal opportunity and the Horatio Alger ideal (If you don't know who Horatio Alger is, ask your American History or English teacher. He has something to do with bootstraps). Americans believe that hard work pays off. If you want to pursue higher education in the United States, there are myriad options to make that a

THE "TEACUP" GENERATION

reality. From community college to open-enrollment, traditional brick-and-mortar institutions to online learning, education is available for those who seek it.

Within all those diverse options emerges a hierarchy regarding the quality of education at one institution over another and which college one ought to attend.

Factors that determine this hierarchy include **geographical biases and familiarity** (the colleges I know are better because I have heard of them), **rankings** (this magazine I bought at the Newark airport Hudson Books before I caught my flight to Cincinnati said it was a "good" school!), and **prestige** (Harvard has been around since 1636 and everyone has heard of it. In a way, Ivy League schools, like the Kardashians, are famous for being famous) all play an overrated and overly influential role in the debate about what constitutes a "good college."

It is remarkable how people always use the modifier *good* to describe colleges instead of *inspiring, life-affirming, rigorous, humanitarian, scientific* or any other word for that matter. This implies that if there are good colleges, ("the ones I know about or am told are good") then there must be some bad colleges out there.

This is not to say that Harvard doesn't provide a tremendous education to its students because, clearly, it has produced a slew of famous (and infamous) graduates—and quite a few successful dropouts too. In *Good Will Hunting*, therapist Sean Maguire reminds us that Ted Kaczynski, the Unabomber, also went to Harvard (Class of 1962).

GET REAL: I have a sneaking suspicion that significant portions of the stunningly large applicant pool at Harvard consist of "why not give it a shot?" applications. Admissions is not a lottery, so the B- student whose uncle is an alum will not get in on that alone, especially since most students who are admitted (and many more who are not) have straight-A averages.

Attending a highly ranked or prestigious college does not necessarily guarantee a happy, successful life; in fact, the colleges that enjoy such acclaim do not possess all— or even the majority of—academic prowess that yields breakthroughs in society.

Moreover, elite colleges do not exist in a vacuum; most faculty members at any institution do not have even one degree from where they currently teach. Therefore, does the perception of prestige and academic quality originate from the degrees and skill of the instructors or the location of their teaching? If prestige comes from earning impressive degrees, then how prestigious are those professors who once taught the faculty? You can see how this chicken-or-egg idea about prestige becomes silly if we just take a step back and examine why we regard institutions in certain ways. When we say that a college is "good," what on earth are we actually saying and how do we measure it? When U.S. News & World Report proclaims that certain schools are "America's Best Colleges," what, specifically, does that mean? Can anyone really rank vastly different institutions on any sort of normal playing field?

And in case you didn't know, the magazine version of U.S. News & World Report ceased to publish in print form in 2010, and the web incarnation exists primarily to maintain that coveted moneymaker: The "Best Colleges" rankings. Numerous publications (some still in print!) have joined the fray to promote their own college rankings, each with a somewhat different priority designed to appeal to those who seek validation for their interest in a school not normally found on the U.S. News list. When colleges appear on any list, you can be certain that current students and alumni will be the first ones to post about it on social media.

- Forbes ranks their Top Colleges by weighing economic factors, primarily "Return on Investment," which takes into account student debt and post-graduate earnings.
- Business Insider looks at "colleges that best prepare their students for success after graduation."
- Princeton Review compiles its list of Happiest Students.
- Kiplinger publishes an annual list of Best Values.
- Money jumped into the crowded field with their own "true-value based" ratings.
- The Economist publishes its list based on "alumni earnings above expectation."
- Even the Department of Education launched the College Scorecard, and although it does not actually rank colleges, it compiles data to assist those who do.

While all these rankings still take exclusivity into account, at least there are finally some alternatives to U.S. News.

Alas, we are only human. We like concrete answers (and we absolutely *love* lists). It seems like everyone wants some kind of pecking order that will let students know where to concentrate their efforts. Although it's quite arbitrary in the grand scheme of things, we cannot resist the fact that when students are admitted to highly selective institutions, it seems to signify something about them. Even though my college counselor heart aches to admit it, it's cool for a student to say, "I got in," especially when thousands (or tens of thousands) did not.

I will never stop saying how stupid and unnecessary rankings are when I see how much stress and drama it causes both families and college counselors, but I will not deny that we like to brag, and we like to compete, and we like to win.

How to Talk to a Teenager about College (Hint: Don't)

Our national fixation with college is why the following scenario plays out year after year, and it is almost assuredly going on right now as you read this.

Listen: A fully grown adult encounters a teenager in any number of settings—classroom, family gathering, workplace, or in line at the Department of Motor Vehicles. What do they have in common? Nothing, perhaps. Sure, they might talk about the weather, sports, or even politics, but eventually the adult will be unable to resist: "Are you in high school? Have you thought about college? Where do you want to go? What do you want to study?"

Asking about college is irresistible, and it annoys the living hell out of the teenagers. Students are bombarded on all sides by enquiring minds who want to know. Part of this prying is natural, understandable, and even forgivable: what *else* would an adult talk to a teenager about?

The unfortunate byproduct of the College Inquisition ("Everyone expects the College Inquisition!") is that the student is overwhelmed and stressed out precisely because *everyone* is asking them the same questions *ad nauseam*. As one of my students observed, seniors don't even like to discuss colleges with each other: "We talk about college for three years, and then during senior year everyone goes silent."

Students know that the college admissions process will evaluate them and how worthy they are. Are they smart enough? Hardworking enough? Strong (mentally and/or physically) enough? Only the admissions process will determine that, or so they believe.

For some students, the college itself is the most important factor, but for others it's the field of study or potential job opportunities that holds sway. Students have to ask themselves, for example, do they really like New York University or do they want to major in business? If your mentality is that you'll only attend UPenn's Wharton School of Business but you have no interest in the renowned business schools at North Carolina, Michigan, or Carnegie Mellon, then you are severely limiting your options.

When it comes to choosing a career, an astounding number of college-bound students are on a pre-med track or other "pre" professional track. Wealthy students, who are third- or fourth-generation college attendees, feel the pressure to major in "something meaningful" (which is code for "get rich"). In addition, first-generation students from lower socioeconomic backgrounds are pressured to select a practical, high-paying major in order to justify the college expense and repay the investment made by their families.

GET REAL: There is no college major called "pre-med." Any major (yes, anything!) can be a considered pre-med. Do the admissions officers a huge favor and stop asking if their college has pre-med. They all do.

Once when I was working in admissions, one of my favorite students came from a pretty weak high school, and he wanted to be a teacher. I fought like crazy for him in committee for the better part of an hour, and I even said some fairly snarky things to the committee (I was actually reprimanded by my supervisor who warned me against tearing up while advocating). After the student was admitted, he emailed me and told me that everyone told him to become a doctor instead of a teacher "because of the chance he was given."

Defending Your Life

Not only does a college-bound teenager have to explain what they want to study but where they aspire to do it. Students should prepare themselves for ill-informed interrogations by well-meaning friends and family regarding the schools under consideration.

The reaction of largely uninformed adults to the hundreds upon hundreds of institutions of higher education where a student may enroll is highly arbitrary and emotional at best, and at worst it can end up damaging the student's psyche. Adults might think they are trying to help, but conversations with students about colleges can undermine a teen's self-worth and lead to any number of negative outcomes.

PRO TIP: If you find yourself engaged in a conversation with a student about colleges, instead of saying, "I've never heard of it," try replying, "Tell me more about it."

Few adults know the workings and features of many (if any) colleges in any sort of meaningful way. It's all popular reputation and word-of-mouth based on little more than name recognition, much like a how a political candidate with a famous name will enjoy early gains in the polls simply because potential voters have heard of the candidate.

FUN FACT: There is actually a psychological term for this phenomenon. The **propaganda effect** states that people are more likely to rate something as true or favorable if they have heard it in the past. Just think how often a particular college is dismissed because "I haven't heard of that school."

Institutional reputation and prestige, as experienced by the masses, is similar. We do not really know why we all regard Harvard so highly, but we all have heard people say, "it's a good school!" To wit: in Season 27 (!) of *The Simpsons,* during one of their famous episodes set in the future, Bart and Lisa talk about inadequacy:

BART
Do you know what it's like to be second-best at anything?
LISA
Yeah, I do! I'm going to Yale!

College counselors like to say that anyone can get a great education virtually anywhere because academic knowledge is not a zero-sum game and no institution (or set of institutions) has a monopoly on scholarship, yet we are often met with skepticism. After all, if a college has a low admit rate and boasts a high academic profile, it must be doing something right. Right?

Academic excellence, as understood by the general public, really comes down to the chatter associated with prestige.

THE PURSUIT OF UNHAPPINESS AND THE PARADOX OF CHOICE

How an Abundance of College Options Makes Everyone Miserable

CHAPTER 3

Freedom of choice is what you got.
Freedom from choice is what you want.

— Devo, "Freedom of Choice"

ONE OF THE ALL-TIME GREATEST neurotic comedians, Richard Lewis, once joked about how his psychiatrist told him that all his happiness was stress-related. This may be the perfect way to explain how such an ultimately joyous event like getting into college can engender so much anxiety along the way. Fortunately for the vast majority of students, the college application process ends with an acceptance letter, but it's the chase that makes so many families miserable.

A mix of misery and entitlement plagues the college application process today. There are approximately 3,000 degree-granting four-year colleges in the United States. And the vast majority of those schools admit the vast majority of their applicants.

But we crave exclusivity. We no longer subscribe to the Groucho Marx theory that we wouldn't want to attend a college who would have someone like us as a student. On the contrary, we want to attend colleges that will admit us—and virtually no one else. We want validation that we belong, and furthermore, that we deserve it.

To help illustrate this point, take a look at some college guides on the market:

- Barron's *Profiles of American Colleges* includes data on more than 1,650 four-year colleges.
- The Princeton Review's *The Best 379 Colleges* culls that list down to the top 15 percent of schools.
- *The Insider's Guide to the Colleges,* by the staff of the Yale Daily News, narrows the focus a bit more, examining just 330 universities.
- *The Fiske Guide to Colleges* profiles over 300 colleges.
- *U.S. News and World Report* annually ranks the Top 200 schools.
- Barron's *Guide to the Most Competitive Colleges* narrows it down to a select 85.
- *Colleges That Change Lives* explores 40 schools, many that go beyond the most obvious elite schools.

Harry Potter and the Prisoner of Applications

In 2012, during a visit to the offices of the New York Times, the editors of my school newspaper met with one of their online editors. A student asked him what kinds of articles they put online when they need to get a boost in page clicks. The response was quick and definitive: Anything on Harry Potter or How to Get Your Kid into an Ivy League School.

That is when I realized why young adults loved the Harry Potter series so much—
J.K. Rowling's books are the ultimate in college wish fulfillment.

EXPECTATION   REALITY

Everyone knows that Hogwarts is the best school for aspiring wizards and witches. Admission is super selective, the campus is beautiful, and it offers a multitude of useful classes (none of which are taught by graduate students). Most importantly, there are no applications or admissions tests. When magical children are born, an enchanted quill simply writes down their names into a giant parchment book, and when they turn eleven years old they are notified of their acceptance either by letter or in person (for those born to Muggles). There is even financial aid available for students like the orphan Tom Riddle.

Sure, we love stories about good and evil, magic wands, dragons, Quidditch, He-Who-Must-Not-Be-Named, Time-Turners, young love, spells, and potions. But what we really want, in our heart of hearts, is recognition for being who we are. What we really need is a place where we can feel a genuine sense of belonging. Hogwarts gives special children the opportunity to live in a magical place where they can learn and live among others like them.

Students dream of a college experience like Hogwarts. They do not want to worry about crafting the perfect résumé, researching and visiting schools, writing essays, being interviewed, or (shudder) getting denied.

GET REAL: Admissions counselors and college counselors do not like to use the verb "rejected," but rather "denied." To *deny* is to disallow, whereas to *reject* is to dismiss as inferior. It's a nuanced preference, but many college counselor hearts ache when they hear students bemoan that they have been rejected.

Application Inflation

Every year the media reports earnestly about students, enabled by the Common App and afflicted with crippling self-doubt, who apply to dozens and dozens of schools.

The National Association for College Admission Counseling (NACAC) reported that 35 percent of first-time college applicants applied to at least seven schools in the fall of 2016. Roughly half that many seniors (17 percent) applied to that many schools in 2005.

The Common App seems to understand that application mania has gotten out of control, so it limits students to 20 colleges, which is still far too many. Students can get around this limit by creating multiple Common Application accounts, but at least they are trying.

GET REAL: In early January, while most college kids are still on winter break, my high school invites a few alumni back to participate in a forum with current high school juniors. These recent high school graduates discuss the college application process and offer up advice for the kids who are fast approaching the moment when they need to make their college decisions. In 2013, the juniors came out of the meeting room in a tizzy because one girl, who was attending Cornell, casually mentioned that she had applied to 18 schools—and only got into two. The takeaway was not that one of our students got into an Ivy League school; the message was: Panic! We have to apply to 18 schools! And we still might not get in!

Back in the 1970s and 1980s, it was considered outrageous to apply to more than a dozen schools. Today it is not uncommon to see students send out 20 or 30 applications (costing $50 to $75 a pop), and there are well-publicized reports of students submitting upwards of 100 applications.

It is virtually impossible to manage applications for 20 highly selective colleges without the benefit of an administrative assistant. Even if all these colleges use the Common App, many will require supplemental essays and forms, not to mention an interview and a campus visit if you want to ensure you've demonstrated interest.

There is a law of diminishing returns when it comes to college applications. At a certain point, **too many applications become counterproductive.**

As a general rule, students should apply to three or four **reach schools**, so there is absolutely no good reason to apply to all eight Ivy League schools. Sure, the Ivies are all located in the northeast and are hyper-selective, but they actually do not have too terribly much in common. It shows a certain naïveté to have all eight institutions on a college list, and it smacks of not knowing what exactly the Ivy League actually is (Surprise! It's an athletic conference!). This perilous pursuit of prestige is almost certainly fueled by parental paranoia.

And do not start with the inevitable and infuriating annual media infatuation that surrounds students who get into all eight Ivy League institutions!

Students should also apply to a handful of **on-target schools**. These are colleges for which student qualifications match the admissions requirements.

To ensure that they do not get shut out, students should apply to at least two or three **safety** or **foundation schools**. Many of these schools offer rolling admissions, so students should not have to wait until late March to discover if they got in somewhere. It astounds me and my college counseling colleagues when a family cannot think of at least a few foundation colleges that are worthy—there are quite literally thousands from which to choose.

Getting the college list down to a manageable number is not easy, but it is vital for everyone's sanity. If you are planning to apply to more than 15 schools, then chances are that your expansive list is part of the reason why you are knee-deep in the crazy.

Application Overkill: A Cautionary Tale

Application insanity reached its peak in 2017 when a senior from a charter school in Memphis, Tennessee, was *accepted by 149 colleges*.

A red flag goes up when a student applies to over 20 schools—but 149 is an entire flag corps.

Fledgling, five-year-old Power Center Academy High School aided and abetted their students to pursue this unwise strategy.

According to her school counselor, the student was given a list of colleges that do not have application fees. In a misguided attempt to "maximize her options," she kept coming in every week to apply to more schools.

She applied to dozens of safety schools in order to find one that would offer the most monetary aid, but that fails to adequately explain why she kept going until she had 149 offers.

It turns out that Power Center Academy encourages students to become Million Dollar Scholars—a dubious distinction that celebrates racking up scholarships from as many schools as possible, even though only one can be used.

One news report gushed that Power Center Academy students "received more than $30 million in scholarship money."

This statistic is deceptive, at best.

Yes, students were *offered* $30 million, but unless they planned to simultaneously enroll in every school offering a scholarship, they could not actually *receive* all that money.

Students should focus on no more than one dozen schools, not twelve dozen (which *is* kind of gross).

One article featured a photo of the Million Dollar Scholar in her graduation regalia, proudly holding one of those oversized checks that are given to pro golfers and game show winners. The amount written on the check is a staggering $7,620,548.

But after crunching the numbers, that means she would receive, on average, approximately $13,000 per year in financial aid per school. That's nice, but it's no reason to stop the presses.

If this student wanted to get a strong financial aid package, why didn't she and her counselor take the time to strategically plan where to apply instead of taking the shotgun approach?

Why had she not made a college decision as of May 26, 2017—over three weeks after the May 1 decision deadline? Why would any high school think it prudent to create a Million Dollar Scholar program for students who met such a pointless quota?

The answer is hidden underneath the clickbait headlines: So schools can claim they are doing a great job.

Power Center Academy is not alone. If you've ever been to a high school commencement or awards ceremony, at some point an administrator is likely to mention that the graduates of Your School have been offered more than $X million in scholarship money.

Repeat: Those totals mean nothing.

Even if she accepted a sizable scholarship, that means about $7.5 million in scholarships would not be available for her use. But it sure sounds impressive if you're a parent considering sending your child to that high school.

This student wasn't applying to highly selective schools, but that's beside the point. There is minimal advantage in applying to so many schools. While the administrators of Power Center Academy might think the Million Dollar Scholar program benefits their educational goals, it will backfire when colleges find out that students are applying to dozens of schools with no intention of actually attending them. Soon those colleges will stop accepting students from schools that misuse their precious counseling resources.

One year later, it happened again. This time a senior from Greensboro, North Carolina, was featured on the local news and numerous publications (including the

New York Times) for getting accepted by 113 schools and amassing more than $4.5 million in merit scholarships.

Even though the Common App limits students to 20 schools, this student also used the Common Black College Application, which got her application seen by 53 historically black colleges and universities. The rest of the applications were sent free of charge to in-state schools during North Carolina's free college application week in mid-October. While she cast an outrageously large net, she only spent $135 on application fees.

Ultimately, this student received a full scholarship worth $28,000 a year to attend Bennett College in her hometown. One of only two historically black colleges for women, Bennett College had been on probation since 2016, and by February 2019, Bennett had lost its appeal to have its accreditation restored.

The Paradox of Choice and The Ultras

In 2004, psychologist Barry Schwartz presented a theory called "The Paradox of Choice."

Listen: You are on a college search road trip. You and your family are hungry. It's time to eat. You haven't seen anything on the road for miles. And you suddenly spy an Arby's (They have the meats!) You do not consult TripAdvisor. You stop. You eat. You move along down the road.

But the scenario is quite different if you arrive at a veritable food oasis. You find everything, from Applebee's to Zaxby's. There is Chipotle and Taco Bell. Chick-fil-A and KFC. Pizza Hut and Pizza Inn and Little Caesar's and Cici's. And every burger place in the known universe.

Suddenly, the choice isn't so simple. Mom felt ill the last time she had a burrito, your brother is boycotting one place due to its stance on same-sex marriage, and your dad has instituted a 30/30 policy on all meals—nothing that costs over $30 or takes more than 30 minutes to eat. You just want something with bacon and a side of fries. Except your sister is vegan and will make gagging noises if she gets a whiff of your pig-murder deathwich.

The Paradox of Choice also applies if you are searching for a new pair of jeans, browsing Netflix, or looking through college lists—you will find clothes, a show, or a school that fits your budget, taste, and interests. In all probability you will like the Lucky Brand jeans, or *Stranger Things,* or Washington University in St. Louis.

But what if you could have done better?

It's that lingering suspicion that if you had just tried on one more pair, clicked on just one more page, or applied to just one more school, you would have found the *perfect* jeans/series/college.

"UM, I GUESS I'LL TRY A BIT OF EVERYTHING"

In their 1980 song "Freedom of Choice" (cited to begin this chapter), Devo recounts an ancient Roman poem about a dog who found two bones: "He picked at one, he licked the other. He went in circles. He dropped dead." There's a metaphor about the college process in there somewhere...

We used to blame the product if we were unhappy, but now we blame ourselves. In short: **Too much choice makes us miserable.**

And the perfect storm of too many options and too much misery is deciding which schools to put on the college list.

So let's just put it out there—**when we talk about Ultra Selective Elite Colleges, we are referring to schools with prestigious national and international reputations that typically accept fewer than 20 percent of their applicants** (some as low as five percent), which is about 25 to 35 schools, depending on your criteria. These are **The Ultras**.

The Ultras could also include West Point, Annapolis, and the Air Force Academy. Go ahead and add some state flagship schools if they are highly selective for both in-state and out-of-state applicants (North Carolina, Michigan, Texas, Virginia, and California to name but a few). Toss in some top small liberal arts colleges (Williams and Amherst) or a STEM school (Harvey Mudd or Stevens Institute) and maybe a college or two with a highly specific course of study that makes it super selective (think Juilliard or Berklee College of Music).

If you go the Full Monty, you are looking at around 40 schools. And somewhere, some kid reading this book is probably going to apply to all of them. Do not be that kid—you will be miserable and in all likelihood wind up with too many or too few options!

In a May 2013 interview with *Time* magazine, Schwartz, a psychology professor at Swarthmore, said, "Applying to more schools just makes everything worse. Assuming you apply to six schools and get into three, it's a hard decision—you beat yourself up and you're full of regret and doubt about whether you made the right choice. If you apply to 15 schools and get into eight, well, all that does is triple the problem. When you have lots of colleges to choose from—even if you make the right choice—you'll spend your time, anytime you have a bad day, thinking at Swarthmore, 'Well, if I was at Yale, I wouldn't be having a day like this.'"

Ultimately, all this choice "ends up undermining people's enthusiasm and then it becomes self-fulfilling."

Even students who fare obscenely well in the college admissions quest can fall victim to the mania. "Their expectations are so exaggerated," said Frank C. Leana, director of college counseling at the Trinity School in Manhattan—back in 1978! "Regardless of what they achieve, it doesn't match the expectations. If they get into three Ivies and turned down by one, suddenly the loss of the fourth is more painful than the job of achieving the three acceptances. They lose all perspective."

Coveting What We See Every Day

The herd mentality is strong when it comes to finding a college. We tend to go with what we know. A 2010 article in The Economist noted, "In a world that celebrates individualism and freedom, many people decide to watch, wear and listen to exactly the same things as everybody else." Or as serial killer Hannibal Lecter succinctly explains to FBI trainee Clarice Starling in *The Silence of the Lambs*, "Do we seek out things to covet? No, we begin by coveting what we see every day."

When searching for a college to attend, students can look at where their parents, siblings and other extended family members went, but beyond that, they will look at the places where other kids from their school have attended—and especially where their classmates are looking. For this very reason, some students feel like they cannot reveal which colleges they are considering, lest someone else from their school gets any ideas and applies to those same schools.

SUBURBAN LEGEND: A Numbers Racket

Everyone says, "There have never been more students applying for fewer spots in the history of the known universe."

The truth is, **there are not more students applying to college, but there are more applications.** While some colleges are in no rush to add more students, plenty of colleges are in a frenzy to build more classrooms and dorms in order to accommodate additional students. Meanwhile, the number of high school graduates has remained flat for several years.

According to the National Student Clearinghouse Research Center, the total number of college applicants has fallen every year from 2013-2018 (between 1 and 2 percent annually), with no increase expected until 2023. And then, between 2026 and 2031, the number of high school graduates is expected to drop by nine percent. So do the math: More spots available in college combined with fewer high school graduates equals more spots available. Even the size of incoming Ivy League classes grew five percent from 2004 to 2014. Getting into college is competitive, but it's not as impossible as some would lead you to believe.

For those who like to stir up the insanity, this logical narrative does not work. It would not get people clicking on articles or buying more books if everyone announced that there were *fewer* people applying to college. Yet this is the case. **There are more applications being filled out, but that is not the same as saying there are more students applying to college.**

Even among the Ultras, there are more spots available. Yale opened two new residential colleges in 2017, which allowed the university to expand the freshman class by 200 students per year (a 15-percent increase), beginning with the Class of 2021. In 2018, however, Dartmouth, the smallest of the Ivies, rejected a proposal to expand its student body by 10 to 25 percent.

The most cynical observers will assume that this college hysteria is a cash grab. After all, one might logically conclude that every application fee helps build more student athletic centers. In 2017, UCLA announced that they received a record 113,409 freshman applications (in addition to roughly 23,000 transfer applicants). At $70 per application, that comes to almost $8 million in fees. And while colleges often waive the application fee for financially disadvantaged students (or to goose their application numbers by further jacking up the number of applicants), that is still a lot of money.

FUN FACT: Most colleges charge a $50 application fee (the average cost is $42 per application). Stanford charges the most ($90 in 2018).

For the student applying to 20 schools, that can cost a family roughly $1,400 in application fees alone. Of course, after factoring in how much it costs to also send those colleges a student's standardized test scores, take college trips, purchase research materials, hire an accountant to get financial aid information together, and pay for test prep classes and tutors, it is no wonder that some families feel like a few more applications could not possibly hurt.

Colleges do spend big bucks to attract students. According to the National Student Clearinghouse, private, nonprofit colleges spend an average of $2,232 to attract just one student while public universities spend $578 and community colleges just $118. Of course, large public schools enroll far more students than their private school counterparts, but it's not an insignificant sum of money.

GET REAL: In 2016, there were 300 colleges and universities with vacancies at the end of admission season, according to NACAC. That number has been rising, up from about 240 schools in 2010. While most of these colleges do not have a prestigious national reputation, in recent years there have been some recognizable names such as Syracuse, Oregon, Oregon State, Missouri, Indiana, Arizona, Arizona State, Marshall, Xavier (OH), Gonzaga, Colorado State, Iowa State and Stetson University.

Even George Costanza Had 47 Girlfriends

In the *Seinfeld* universe, Jerry and George had a lot of girlfriends, yet inevitably they would find fault with these women and call it off. In the span of 172 episodes, Jerry had 66 different girlfriends. And the nebbish George? He had 47 over nine seasons.

When it comes to narrowing down that monster college list, students need to be more selective. To use a Tinder metaphor, they need to swipe left a whole lot more frequently. But if you feel like the colleges have all the control in the college process, remember:

Two out of the three parts of the college search are in your control. You will decide where to apply and you will decide which offer to take among the schools that accept you.

Success is not the number of times you say YES it's the number of times you say NO. Colleges know this, and the more students they deny, the more people want to apply.

In 2017, colleges accepted 66 percent of first-time freshman applicants. And if you look at the Ultras, many of them once upon a time (like the 1980s) accepted well over one-third of their applicants. Now acceptance rates are in the single digits.

Speaking of the Big Eighties, for a time there was a spate of celebrity couples in which the wife was demonstrably more attractive than the husband (look up Jeff Goldblum & Geena Davis or Billy Joel & Christie Brinkley). Today the term for this phenomenon is Outkicking Your Coverage. If you ask parents, a lot of them will confess that they would probably never be able to get into their alma mater today. They all think they outkicked their coverage.

When students chase the same schools as everyone else, they are not always looking for the best fit, be it academically, financially, or socially. Sometimes it just depends on the food.

THE IMITATION GAME

Trying to Crack the College Code

CHAPTER 4

Although your mind's opaque
Try thinking more if just for your own sake.

— *The Beatles, "Think for Yourself"*

U NLESS YOU HAVE WORKED in the espionage community or for the New England Patriots, nothing will prepare you for a true cloak-and-dagger experience quite like applying to college.

Everyone thinks there is a secret formula for getting in, and the unfortunate victims are the students who have to jump through real and metaphorical hoops in order to create (on paper) the ideal applicant.

In Chapter 12, we will look at what takes place at the college level, but this chapter looks at what happens in the high schools.

The Quest for the Secret Handshake

There is no conspiracy theory too absurd for those who are looking for a leg up with the admissions committee (at one university there was a spate of copycat applicants who mailed admissions officers a shoe, hoping that it would help them "get their foot in the door"). It's what one academic dean calls "The Quest for the Secret Handshake."

If you think such over-the-top techniques are rare, think again.

During application season, seemingly reasonable parents will refuse to discuss where their kids are applying because they fear other parents will decide to have their kids apply there as well and somehow "take their spot."

Once on *Seinfeld*, George Costanza mentioned to his girlfriend Susan that he wanted to name his firstborn child Seven. She nixes the idea and then mentions it in passing to her cousin and husband, who are expecting their first child. Of course, they love the name for their daughter. George loses his mind when they announce they are naming their baby Seven, and he even follows the couple to the hospital, trying to convince them to use the name Soda instead.

Compared to some parents, George Costanza is the model of restraint.

SUBURBAN LEGEND: Limited Possibilities

One of the most common myths is the notion that a certain college will only accept a finite number of students from a particular high school. Thus, students (and their families) will fixate on the handful (or couple dozen) of students who are also applying from a given high school and assume that they have to be better than them for admittance. This popular admissions myth almost certainly emanates from someone who said, "They don't want to admit too many kids from one school!" This is simply not the case. Admissions offices do not limit how many students they will admit from any given high school. Are students in competition? Yes, but students are competing in the national application pool, not just from one high school.

"THESE REMIND ME OF
MY APPLICANTS"

Everything Is a Copy of a Copy of a Copy

Whether it's Alan Turing trying to crack the German Enigma Machine or MIT card sharks trying to beat the Vegas blackjack tables, everyone is looking for the winning formula. Even Facebook began as an algorithm at Harvard to rate the attractiveness of coeds.

Students often compare the college admissions process to *Game of Thrones* or *The Hunger Games* because it's full of cutthroat competition and everyone is looking to ensure that the odds are forever in their favor.

One could also look to Omar Little from *The Wire* to sum up the situation: "The game's out there, and it's play or get played. That simple."

Instead of coming up with convoluted schemes to get into these highly competitive schools, parents and students should spend more time researching what they actually want from a college and then allow kids the space to do what they want in order to prepare themselves for college.

True Story: A student from the Class of 2013 was admitted to Harvard. An Asian-American, she was near the top of her class, was a nationally recognized painter and an accomplished dancer. For most of her life, she attended weekend dance classes. When she went back to visit some of her instructors, she was astonished to learn that for two years, the parents of younger students were trying to have their kids replicate her life. It was a discovery that "both flattered and creeped me out," she admitted.

One night while out at dinner with her family, a 10-year-old girl walked up to her table just to meet her. The young girl knew this Harvard student by name, but they had never met. In her neighborhood, she was a rock star, and she regularly turned down offers to host dinner parties for families of aspiring Harvard applicants—many of whom were still in elementary school!

The Merits of a Meritocracy

Most college applicants agree that college admissions should be a meritocracy, but over the years minorities have become a convenient scapegoat for those who don't get in where they want. If admissions were truly a meritocracy, then Asian students might be admitted at the rates seen at Caltech, where the undergraduate student body in the fall of 2018 was 40 percent Asian and 27 percent White. Suddenly, people are not quite as in favor of merit-based admissions as they once claimed.

Caltech is an outlier. They have no preferential treatment for legacies, athletes, or donors—and they do not use a quota system. Consequently, their student body has double the percentage of Asians as virtually any other Ultra.

In 2018, Harvard went to court to defend its admission policies because a supposed quota system curtailed the number of accomplished Asian students who are hampered by being held to a higher standard than other students. The role of race in college admissions hangs in the balance until the Supreme Court likely takes up this case at a later date.

One glaring problem for many highly qualified students, regardless of ethnicity or background, is that their applications tend to have a sameness that makes it difficult to stand out from the crowd.

Sheer Linsanity

For one Asian-American applicant, NBA veteran Jeremy Lin, Harvard was a fallback option.

In 2012, Lin became a global sensation as a member of the New York Knicks during a spectacular February that spawned "Linsanity" and landed him on the cover of *Sports Illustrated*. He parlayed that magical run into a three-year, $25-million contract with the Houston Rockets.

Lin, who hailed from Palo Alto, California, sent his résumé and highlights DVD to every Ivy League school, UCLA, and his dream school—Stanford. Only Harvard and Brown guaranteed him a spot on the basketball team, so he chose to take his talents to Cambridge.

It's tough to get into Harvard. It's also tough to play collegiate basketball. But with excellent grades and athletic skills, you have a better than average chance. Jeremy Lin was not trying to imitate anyone else to get into Harvard (there were no other American-born Asian NBA stars to emulate)—he just wanted to play basketball and had the credentials and skills to make it possible.

Colleges are trying to build a diverse environment, and if all they admitted were female classics majors who excelled in lacrosse and debate, then they would not have a diverse freshman class.

The simple solution for students who are prone to imitation is to be the best version of themselves. Do not try to replicate what might have worked for someone else.

If Everyone Jumped off a Bridge

In 2015, the conventional wisdom went something like this: *With all the changes and uncertainty surrounding the newly revamped SAT, seniors should take the ACT.*

This was the advice that most college counselors recommended when nervous families were trying to decide whether to have their students prepare for the ACT or the "new" SAT in 2015-2016. The prevailing opinion was that taking the updated SAT was simply too risky, so students were advised to play it safe, follow the crowd, and register for the ACT. *[Read more about the battle for testing hegemony between the SAT and ACT in Chapter 6.]*

And then the results came out in August 2016: the average composite ACT score dropped 0.2 points to a 20.8—the lowest score in five years. Because the percentage of students taking the ACT rose from 52 percent in 2014 to 64 percent for the class of 2016, it ended up driving down the scores.

Even more troubling data came from the ACT's own report "The Condition of College & Career Readiness": Among 2016 ACT-tested graduates, 38 percent of students had a "strong readiness of college coursework" (down two percent), and 34 percent of students did not meet any of the benchmark scores and were deemed "likely to struggle in first-year college courses" (up three percent).

So remember, **when everyone tries to use the same strategy, it can backfire**.

Cheat Codes

Here is a strategy that some try: don't apply for the major that you are really interested in because it is too competitive. The rationalization is that students can apply for an easier program and then transfer into the department they really want once they get admitted.

One aspect of applications that becomes clear once you actually fill out the forms is that, for a number of universities, you are not really applying to a university—you are applying to a college within the university: Social Science, Music, Architecture, etcetera. These days, Engineering and Business Schools are two of the most challenging from an admissions perspective, so people look for the backdoor entry by applying to a division perceived as less challenging, like Communications.

Transferring is often difficult, and you are not doing yourself any favors by trying to game the system based on specious reasoning. Due to tight curriculum mapping, if you transfer from one program to another, then you might not be able to graduate in four years, which is potentially another $50,000 you have to spend just because you did not apply for what you wanted to study in the first place. **Instead of looking for a "college hack," you very well might have gotten in on your own merits and saved yourself a lot of time, money, and aggravation.**

GET REAL: It is easier to transfer out of a popular program than into one.

The English department at my high school offers seniors their choice of semester-long college-style seminars. Seniors are asked to rank their top choices in order to get the course they want. We offer a wide range of classes from which to choose: Shakespeare, Graphic Novels, Memoir, and Science-Fiction, to name but a few.

Every year I have some students who tell me how much they want to take my American Pop Culture class, so I advise them to mark it as their first choice. Then I see their forms—and many have my class ranked No. 2—so invariably they get sorted into their top choice. Later, when I tell them that they didn't get my class because they listed it second, they look surprised and say that they put it second because they heard that no one ever gets their first choice.

It boggles the mind that otherwise smart kids would overlook this logical fallacy: If nobody got their first choice, there would be a mutiny. Somewhere, deep in the teenage brain, there must exist a kind of perverse logic in which students would rather accomplish something the wrong way, odds be damned, than do it the right way.

A Midsummer's College Program

Ask high school students about what kind of mail they get from colleges, and you will inevitably hear about countless promotional materials for summer academic programs hosted at all the best colleges. Some of these summer programs last a week while others can run a month. These programs are often marketed to appear highly selective (some really are), and the perception is that attending one of these programs will increase the likelihood of admission down the road. Parents often make this assumption: "My son has been going to the University of Dream School's Summer Study Spectacular since he was seven! They're going to see how brilliant he is and get to know him so well!"

The number of these programs has gone up exponentially over the last few decades. And why not? These institutions have world-class facilities and faculty, and the vast majority of their college students have gone home for the summer. Thus there are lots of empty campuses, and colleges need to figure out how to pay those expensive summer electric bills.

Attending summer enrichment programs can be an excellent way to explore a college campus, both in the classroom and residence halls (unless the program sticks the kids in the worst dorms without air conditioning). Additionally, high school students engage in classroom learning, group work, academic contests, and the like—all things worth celebrating—but families need to understand that these programs are totally separate from the admissions office and are often run by academic departments for the purpose of replenishing their budget.

GET REAL: About half my students who ask me about college summer programs assume it will help them get admitted at the host institution, but this is seldom the case. When I gently explain how it really works, they usually respond, "I don't want to do it if it won't help me get in."

When it comes to deciding what to do during the summer, there has to be a better way. Fortunately, there is. Some of the most compelling summer experiences I have seen involve *student-created* experiences: An internship, volunteer work, or even a good old-fashioned summer job are all fantastic options that cost little to nothing or even allow students to turn a profit. Think about starting a small business (e.g., lawn care, babysitting, tutoring), partnering with a non-profit organization, shadowing a professional with a job you might like to pursue, or working at your local movie theater. And they make great essay topics, every single one!

International Applicants of Mystery

At most institutions, international students typically do not qualify for need-based financial aid, but they can apply for merit-based scholarships. More institutions are starting to offer need-based financial aid to international students, but it's still only a handful.

The upshot is that the high-achieving international student who *is* admissible might not be admitted *if* they have financial need. My college once had to waitlist a strong Canadian applicant who was living in the U.S. because he had significant financial need.

Secondly, international students whose native language isn't English have to take the Test of English as a Foreign Language (TOEFL). This exam will often sink many students. Otherwise, evaluating international student is not all that different from assessing American students.

International students provide a budgetary cushion for smaller and mid-sized universities since they pay full freight, but in 2016 a combination of stricter U.S. immigration policies and anti-foreigner rhetoric resulted in a decline of new international students enrolled in American colleges for the first time in 12 years.

While American colleges saw a decline in international student enrollment of three percent, other countries have seen a boost in foreign applicants, including Canada (18 percent), Spain (25 percent), Japan (13 percent), China (11 percent), and New Zealand (34 percent).

If you have dual citizenship with the United States and any other nation, then you are in great shape. As an American, you can qualify for need-based financial aid, and you count toward the school's international admission numbers!

If you look at any college profile, you will often see a chart indicating where students from different nations come from, and it will always be followed by an asterisk to indicate that this list includes dual citizens. Thus, if you are dual citizen, then you are likely helping to meet the school's institutional goal of having international students. You still need to demonstrate strong academics and whatever else you have going for you, but your citizenship status is a definite plus.

The Cold War Ended, So the Climbing Wall Arms Race Started

Students aren't the only ones prone to imitation.

There is a movement within higher education (state schools in particular) to load up on expensive amenities and fancy dorms in order to lure out-of-state students who have better test scores than the in-state crowd *and* who have the wherewithal to pay full tuition.

Part of the reason for this trend is that during the Cold War era, colleges and universities did not have to compete like they do in the current landscape of higher education. Back then, the federal government was happy to fund research while students and parents had reasonable or low expectations about student services, residence halls, and food—and few students traveled all that far away to attend college.

Today, students and families have enormously high expectations for student life, teaching, career centers, residence halls, dining, and the like (*check out the 3D printers we get to use!*). Institutions can no longer offer powdered eggs in the dining hall, and they have to find ways to woo the out-of-state vegan student who wants to do yoga every morning before having their dirty clothes picked up by the college's on-campus laundry service.

Colleges are now touting far more than their academics, especially the quality of life that a student will have as they pursue their studies. These creature comforts have become a baseline expectation in the mind of many in Generation Z. In 2015, the *Boston Globe* explored the high (and often unreasonable) expectations for what a college will provide, ranging from the quality of the buildings and dorms to the diverse food choices. It's a new paradigm in college recruiting, and schools are discovering that the arms race has become a Catch-22 proposition.

Malcolm Gladwell (*Outliers, David & Goliath*) has waged his own crusade against the imbalance between the haves and have-nots in the world of higher education. In a three-part investigation on his *Revisionist History* podcast in 2016, Gladwell challenged some established business practices.

In one episode ("Food Fight"), Gladwell highlights the way two similar colleges, Bowdoin in Maine and Vassar in New York, handle their on-campus food options. Bowdoin provides first-class culinary options from locally sourced farms (including lobster) while Vassar's food is, well, uninspiring. The ethical trade-off, according to Gladwell, is that Vassar enrolls twice as many low-income students on Pell grants as Bowdoin. If Vassar accepted more students willing to pay full price, he reasons, they could use the surplus to invest more money in the cafeteria, but Gladwell wants to see colleges invest more in poor students than luxury features. Vassar made the conscious decision to increase the number of low-income students, from seven percent for the incoming class of 2006 to a peak of 24 percent in 2014. Such a concerted effort required the reallocation of resources, and at Vassar, the food is not a top priority.

A stunning case study of student amenity excess can be found at the University of Missouri. In 2005, Mizzou opened a nearly $40-million student recreation center, which featured an indoor beach club complete with whirlpools, waterfalls, and a lazy river. In May 2016, Mizzou announced that enrollment had declined by 2,600 students, resulting in a loss of $36 million in tuition revenue. The next year, roughly 5,000 fewer students applied.

Part of the budget shortfall is due to Mizzou attracting fewer out-of-state students—even with the state-of-the-art MizzouRec to entice them. According to the university, 40 percent of Mizzou students had typically come from out-of-state, but the number fell to 33 percent.

In November 2015, weeks of escalating student protests at Mizzou eventually led to the ouster of the university president and campus chancellor. While a victory for students, the negative publicity hastened an already declining application pool, resulting in a 35-percent drop in all applications in just two years. Budget cuts soon followed, including the decision in July 2017 to close a medical research institute that had cost $10 million to build and was less than ten years old. Meanwhile, some now-empty dormitories are being rented out for $120 a night for events like homecoming and fall family visit weekend. By 2018, the total number of applicants to Mizzou had rebounded (up 12.2 percent), but the number of students actually enrolling continues to decline (down over 2,000 students in 2017).

The financial difficulties at Mizzou are not uncommon across the country. In 2018, Moody's Investor Service said that revenues at state-run colleges had increased 2.9 percent while expenses rose 4.9 percent—the second year in a row indicating a revenue shortfall.

FUN FACT: According to the ACT, students who score best on their test (scores ranging from 33 to 36) attend colleges farther away from home—an average of 172 miles—while those who score the national average of 20.8 will journey around 45 miles.

Team Coco and Late Night Icons

On June 12, 2011, comedian Conan O'Brien gave the commencement address at Dartmouth, the first time he had given a graduation speech since he spoke to the Class of 2000 at Harvard, his alma mater.

Near the end of his speech to the Dartmouth graduates, O'Brien discussed the history of late-night television hosts:

> Way back in the 1940s there was a very, very funny man named Jack Benny. He was a giant star, easily one of the greatest comedians of his generation. And a much younger man named Johnny Carson wanted very much to be Jack Benny. In some ways he was, but in many ways he wasn't. He emulated Jack Benny, but his own quirks and mannerisms, along with a changing medium, pulled him in a different direction. And yet his failure to completely become his hero made him the funniest person of his generation. David Letterman wanted to be Johnny Carson, and was not, and as a result my generation of comedians wanted to be David Letterman. And none of us are. My peers and I have all missed that mark in a

thousand different ways. But the point is this: It is our failure to become our perceived ideal that ultimately defines us and makes us unique. It's not easy, but if you accept your misfortune and handle it right, your perceived failure can become a catalyst for profound reinvention.

So whether you are an aspiring comedian or college applicant—or both—it is incumbent on you to find those you wish to emulate, but do not sacrifice who you are in the process.

COMING ATTRACTIONS

How Movie Trailers Are Like College Applications

CHAPTER 5

Everybody's a dreamer and everybody's a star,
And everybody's in show biz, it doesn't matter who you are.

— *The Kinks, "Celluloid Heroes"*

B ACK IN 1982, I went to the local mall to watch a movie with some friends. What movie we went to see wasn't important (the forgettable medical comedy *Young Doctors in Love*)—we were there to watch the trailers. Specifically one highly anticipated movie preview.

Before the feature film, 20th Century Fox was showing an advance trailer for the third installment of the Star Wars saga: *Return of the Jedi*. We could hardly wait until Memorial Day Weekend 1983, so the trailer was all that would tide us over until then. After an assortment of other previews, the familiar John Williams fanfare let us know to focus our attention, then the announcer told us to "return for the climactic clash between the forces of good and evil."

Everyone was back—Luke Skywalker was dressed in black, standing above the Sarlaac Pit. Princess Leia was in a gold outfit that would fuel the fantasies of a generation of young boys. Han and Lando were looking suave as always. R2-D2 and C-3PO were along for the ride. And Darth Vader was as menacing as ever. There were even some fuzzy woodland creatures running around that looked suspiciously like George Lucas.

When the feature film was over (an unsuccessful attempt to replicate *Airplane!* humor), instead of leaving, we remained in the darkened theater for 20 minutes to watch the movie trailers again. After we had seen the *Jedi* preview a second time, we got up and left. There were probably a few confused patrons who wondered why we weren't staying for the feature film.

Like many movie fans, I always want to arrive early because I love previews—the more the better. I recently watched 22 minutes of trailers before a film.

In the 1980s, you would see the occasional TV commercial for an upcoming movie, but they were typically only 30 seconds long. Movie trailers in the theater were often over two minutes. In the era before *Rotten Tomatoes*, I would compute the mental math in order to determine if a movie was worthy of going to see in the theaters, waiting for it to come out on video, watching it on basic cable, or skipping it altogether.

A good movie trailer makes you want to see the film immediately. You do not want to wait. Like Veruca Salt demanding a goose that lays golden eggs, you want it *now*. The best movie trailers give you a sense of anticipation (think *The Dark Knight, Black Panther, Independence Day* and *Pulp Fiction*). They give you the feeling that you might see something new, something different. Watching those trailers makes you feel like those movies are more worthy than every other film being released.

Sure, sometimes the movies fail to fulfill the promise of the trailers (I'm looking at you, *Cloverfield* and *Watchmen),* but they definitely get people talking. A mediocre trailer simply does not get you fired up to see a film. It's all about marketing.

How to Market Yourself

The full application folder should give colleges a glimpse at the quality of the applicant. Admissions officers cannot hang out with you throughout high school, so you need to give them the highlights the same way a movie trailer has to deliver the gist of a full-length feature in just two minutes.

Have you noticed that advance movie posters will start to appear more than a year before the film's release? Sometimes studios will release teaser trailers to whet your appetite, often with just a few seconds of footage.

That is what it's like for students during their sophomore and especially junior year of high school. Once you take your practice PSAT test in October of 10th grade, you will be inundated by mail from colleges. Your email inbox and your home mailbox alike will be bursting with flattering statements about your potential.

The Dark Arts of College Admissions

Colleges hire sorcerers (or technology people—same difference) to track whether or not students are opening all those email invitations or replying to the postcards with personalized account numbers.

Here's why:

Colleges need you to apply. The more students who apply, the more students they can deny, and the lower the admission rates. Lower admit rates = more prestige.

But these days it's not enough to have historically low admission rates. Yes, it looks good if the college is perceived as exclusive, but in the world of the Common App and trophy hunting and students who apply to 20 or more colleges, a school can have an accept rate under 20 percent and still have two-thirds of its accepted students enroll somewhere else—and those are *good* numbers!

Harvard and Stanford set the bar at over 80 percent yield, UPenn and Princeton yield just under two-thirds of their accepted students, and Vanderbilt and Georgetown net just under 50 percent. As a benchmark, the Ultras have a yield between 45 and 75 percent, and according to U.S. News and World Report, the average Liberal Arts College has a yield of just over 29 percent. NACAC reports that overall yield is around 36 percent, which is down 13 percent since 2002. In order to manage their yield, colleges can defer students or place them on the waitlist.

In 2015, Drexel University in Philadelphia had seen its yield drop from around 32 percent to a paltry 8 percent despite receiving a record number of applications (an increase of about 300 percent in just nine years). With a yield that low, Drexel had to accept nearly 80 percent of its applicants just to fill its freshman class each year. Drexel re-evaluated all the shortcuts they were offering to applicants, like Fast App, which made it super easy for students to apply but gave them little or no incentive to enroll after getting accepted. To fix their low yield, Drexel got back to sending its representatives into high schools and actually meeting with students in order to foster relationships and increase the likelihood that those who apply will actually enroll. In 2014, they made 75 visits to high schools, college fairs and receptions. One year later, they made 1,375 such visits, and their yield almost doubled to 15.8 percent.

Remember, in the college process, **students control two-thirds of the variables: where to apply and where to attend after all options are presented. The schools control the other part of the equation by deciding who gets admitted.**

(1) Schools spend millions to entice students to apply. That gives them a **pool of applicants.**

(2) Schools decide who gets in, which determines the **admission rate.**

(3) Students decide where to go, which sets the **yield.**

Students have to market themselves to the colleges to get in, but once the acceptance letters get sent, it's time for the colleges to persuade the students to accept their offer.

Of course, colleges secure a sizable percentage of their accepted students through the Early Decision process, which reduces the need for colleges to lock down the students accepted through the Early Action or Regular Decision process.

Schools vary in their approach to getting students to choose them, from using social media, sending impressive acceptance notifications, giving students swag (including t-shirts, flash drives, and an assortment of gadgets emblazoned with the college logo), or inviting students to attend local social events and on-campus programs. Some schools even pay for airfare and hotel costs (just ask!). And, of course, the financial aid package plays a significant role in determining who will accept.

Much in the same way that students would like to know that colleges truly want them to apply, some colleges want to know the sincerity of student interest.

Despite the incredible shrinking yield, those numbers have been fairly constant in recent years, which is good for the colleges because a change of more than one percent can have significant repercussions.

If more students than expected decide to accept, there may not be enough housing, courses, or instructors to meet the demand. It's a lot like when an airline overbooks a plane. In the end, schools utilize an algorithm to determine the exact number of students to accept, but if the projections are inaccurate, it can cost the college. With airline carriers, sometimes passengers are bumped to first class while others are given flight vouchers and other incentives to persuade customers to take a later flight.

In 2012, Case Western in Cleveland had 30 percent more students accept their admissions offer than expected, which resulted in a shortage of dorm rooms and available courses.

Sometimes, having an unexpectedly high yield can have a happy ending. One of my former students was accepted to a medical school that had more students accept their placement than they could handle, so they offered to waive four years of tuition for students who were willing to defer med school for just one year. While it did mean living at home with mom and dad after graduating from college, she was able to finish medical school without crushing student loan debt.

On the flip side, when UC Irvine was faced with 850 too many incoming freshman in the fall of 2017, they took a hardline stand by informing 500 students that their offer of admission had been withdrawn a mere two months before the start of the fall term. According to campus data, 290 cases were due to transcript-related issues and the others were for poor senior grades.

Unless a student fails a required class, most colleges overlook transgressions such as a stray D or a housing form that is a few days late. Rescinding admission is rare—in 2017, UC San Diego revoked nine offers and UCLA withdrew seven, while the University of Texas at Austin had none.

From a publicity standpoint, UC Irvine chose to handle the situation in much the same way United Airlines did in forcefully removing a screaming passenger from a plane in April 2017. In both cases, it was ugly.

The UC Irvine decision—which was met by outrage from the college counseling community—underscores some important issues within college admissions:

(1) While some schools can absorb extra students with creative scheduling and housing options, many large public institutions like UC Irvine only receive funding for a specific number of students each year. If colleges go above that total, it comes out of their end, so it's easier to get rid of students who have not yet matriculated than make cuts that affect the rest of the university.

(2) Do not let Senioritis derail your college plans. While it is still rare for colleges to rescind admission due to a single D, when schools are faced with tough choices, a poor grade that might get overlooked at one school can provide just the solution for a college that needs to fix an overcrowding problem. Because it's common for students who have been accepted into college to display signs of Senioritis, many private schools send out a "Fear of God" letter, warning students that continued poor performance down the home stretch could jeopardize their conditional offer of admission. These letters are usually a cause for alarm, not panic, as long as you get your act together before it's too late.

(3) Do not miss deadlines for final transcripts, housing, or anything else. If sending materials yourself, be sure to purchase postage that includes delivery confirmation, just in case there are any snafus.

PRO TIP: If you are not prepared for years of faceless, nameless bureaucracy with inflexible and capricious rules, then a large state school might not be right for you.

Can't Hardly Wait

On the other end of the spectrum, if the yield is lower than expected, then the colleges have to make up for the shortage by pulling students off the waitlist. Colleges cannot just take the first name off the waitlist. If a music student declines an offer, then colleges look for a musician.

As you can imagine, the more selective the school, the more unlikely it is that you will get off the waitlist. What's sometimes shocking to students is just how many applicants are placed on the waitlist, even if they have virtually no chance of getting in.

With just a cursory glance at some statistics, you can see the numbers game at work. In 2014, Caltech accepted 576 students and put 615 on the waitlist. And of those, 482 accepted a spot on the waitlist, from which only 47 students were eventually granted admission. And that's the good news because Caltech took no one off the waitlist in 2012, 2013, or 2015.

Also in 2014, Dartmouth accepted 2,220 students and 1,152 chose to enroll, which meant none of the 1,855 students on the waitlist got in.

All this data is available on the College Board website. Even though some colleges do not publicize their waitlist data, it should not be too difficult to determine the odds based on the data from comparable schools. Want more waitlist data? The following trio of numbers represents (1) the number of students who were offered a spot on the waitlist, (2) how many accepted a spot on the waitlist, and (3) how many got accepted from the waitlist in the 2015–2016 academic year:

	Offered Waitlist	Put on Waitlist	Accepted from Waitlist
Vanderbilt	6,016	1,736	209
Rice	2,158	1,256	150
UPenn	2,651	1,600	136
Cornell	3,143	2,026	96
Amherst	1,341	600	61
Princeton	1,138	818	41
Stanford	958	695	7

Waitlist activity ebbs and flows. When parents and students inevitably ask, "How many students do you expect to take from the waitlist?" you should already know that it depends. And it mostly depends on how many students accept the initial offers of admission. In 2014, Johns Hopkins admitted one student from the waitlist, but in 2015 they took 187. Similarly, UC Davis went from 12 waitlist admits in 2014 to over 2,000 the next year. Meanwhile, Georgia Tech had 174 in 2014 but only 38 the following year, and Carnegie Mellon dropped from 73 to 4 over the same period.

The waitlist numbers can go way up for large public schools, but there is just as much volatility in how many students ultimately enroll. In 2015, Penn State admitted virtually everyone from its waitlist (1,445 of 1,473) after taking none the year before, while rival Ohio State let in all waitlisted students in 2014 and 2015.

SUBURBAN LEGEND: Special Deliveries

Since colleges send promotional materials to students, there are people who think it is a good idea for students to send admissions officers some goodies in return.

Schools are often inundated by not-so-clever ploys. Most schools will state on their website that students should not send additional materials, but there are some, notably Harvard, that do allow it. If you are considering sending something extra, it is almost certainly a bad idea. **You might think a thick student folder is a positive, but it is actually counterproductive in admissions.**

When the Juice Isn't Worth the Squeeze: The Epic Saga of Lime Girl

The story you are about to read is true. The names have been changed to protect the applicant.

I was assigned Tampa Bay and the West Coast of Florida as part my admissions territory at Vanderbilt. I found many wonderful high schools, college counselors, and students there. At one high school, two girls had applied Early Decision. I had met them during my visit, and I found them both quite likable. That's not the reason they were admitted, but it is always nice to accept students you like.

Sure enough, they were strong Early Decision admits, but they might not have gotten in during the more competitive Regular Decision pool. Still, they were wonderful students that we were happy to welcome to our freshman class.

Some of their classmates applied Regular Decision, and one girl (the protagonist of our story) was eventually waitlisted.

Soon after notifications went out, my phone rang.

"This is her top choice!" mom exclaimed. "We can't believe she has been waitlisted! This is a nightmare!"

I listened patiently, tried to explain the selectivity of the pool, and reassured the mother that everything would be fine (not clearly defining what "fine" meant since I was unsure myself).

I was also a little confused. If her daughter was so certain that we were her top choice, then why did she not apply Early Decision? Maybe she decided that she *really* loved us *after* she applied. Maybe it was a financial concern. Or maybe mom was making this same phone call to all the other colleges that had waitlisted her daughter.

Then mom claims, "Two other students took *her* spot at ED!"

Like most high schools, everyone is up in everyone else's business. Students and parents gossip more than middle school kids at lunch.

I explained to her that there were no quotas within a given high school, and I certainly could not speak to her about other students out of concern for confidentiality.

Mom was not buying it. While she was more tears than pitchforks, *her* daughter was slighted, and those *other* students took *her* daughter's spot, so instinctively she *had* to call.

Later that day, I contacted the counselor at her high school—not to complain about the mom (or to scheme about admissions decisions), but just to let him know what was going on. He understood and appreciated the call.

Flash forward a few weeks. I get a call from the mailroom: "You have a package from Florida." My mind raced to determine who could have sent it.

I went downstairs and was presented with a box of two dozen key limes as well as a folder containing a detailed history of the key lime, a letter from a student (at least it was signed by her), and an odd photo that I gathered was the student's senior portrait.

Sure enough, the whole package was from the student whose mother was decrying her daughter's placement on the waitlist.

I read the history of the key lime (which was actually pretty fascinating) and the accompanying letter, which was basically a reiteration of her mom's phone call but in more reverent prose: "I hope I didn't hurt my chances by not applying ED[1]. This is my top choice[2]. If there is anything I can do to improve my chances, please let me know[3]."

Then I discovered that she had sent our director of admissions a similar package. Our director was known for stopping committee meetings in order to Google the namesake of high schools named after historical figures just so he could learn more about the applicant's school.

"This is really *interesting*!" my director proclaimed, clearly amused. "Did you know the key lime originated in Southeast Asia?"

I called her high school counselor again.

"Your students are sending me produce!"

The counselor was somewhat chagrined, chuckled gently, and apologized. I explained that he didn't need to apologize; I just didn't want students to send fruit every time they got waitlisted.

A few weeks later, I looked at the report of students who had been admitted off the waitlist. These decisions fill institutional needs, and the higher-ups on the staff make those decisions. *Lime Girl was being offered admission!* I immediately went to my Director.

"You realize you admitted Lime Girl."

"Yeah, have fun with that," he confirmed.

One of the best things an admissions officer gets to do is tell students they have been admitted off the waitlist. Typically, this is done by calling the student and offering them a place in the class. Sometimes they politely (or not) decline and say they are enrolling elsewhere, but usually it's absolute euphoria.

Not knowing quite what to expect in this instance, I called Lime Girl.

After identifying myself, I felt compelled to preface the big news: "I'm going to ask you something, but before I do, I want you to know that this had nothing to do with the limes you sent. That was very nice of you, but that does not have anything to do with why you were admitted," I said. "So, would you like to come to Vanderbilt?"

After a pregnant pause, she meekly replied with all the excitement of a comatose mime, "Yeah. Totally."

"Are you happy?"

---

[1] you did

[2] awesome?

[3] it's certainly not sending me the history of citrus

"Yeah."

"Well, congratulations!"

I knew that her mom, who had continued to call and email me for weeks to see if her daughter was coming off the waitlist, would just *love* to hear the good news. I naïvely presumed that Lime Girl would immediately call her mother to celebrate, so I waited an hour and then put in a call to mom, just to make it official. I half expected that she would call me first.

The phone rang. Mom answers. When I tell her who I am, she starts panting loudly, as if I am about to give her very good news or very bad news.

"Did your daughter call you?"

"No!?" she said with trepidation. (How do you not call your mom and tell her you got in?) "We're offering her admission."

Mom's reaction was the exact opposite of her daughter's. "Wow! This is her dream! This is amazing! Thank you, thank you, thank you!" And so on.

I mentioned the limes and how I thought that was "different."

"Well, we (cue the eye-roll when parents say *we*) thought it would be fun to show you part of her hometown."

Epilogue: Lime Girl enrolled. During the fall, I was out traveling my territory, recruiting the next class of students. Travel often has admissions officers on the road for weeks at a time. When I returned to my desk, there was a grocery bag with a note from Lime Girl attached. This time: lemons! Unfortunately, because they had been sitting on my desk for weeks, they had developed a thick layer of mold.

When life gives you moldy lemons, what can you do?

My Aim Is True: Demonstrating Interest

So what does all this **demonstrated interest** have to do with admissions?

The simplest way to explain demonstrated interest is quite vague and as follows: More selective colleges (i.e., the Ultras) are less likely to care, yet some care within a geographic context (visit the colleges that are easy to get to), while some do not care at all. Oh, and public institutions are less likely to care than private.

For the Ivy Leagues and the other Ultras with a high yield, demonstrated interest usually does not help one get admitted. Sure, visiting a school and taking a tour might help you decide whether or not to apply, but many of those colleges do not take your interest into account when selecting their freshman class.

Which schools *do* take demonstrated interest into account? Generally speaking any school that's not an Ultra or a Big State School. If Washington University in St. Louis, Tufts, Rice, Emory or Tulane is your top choice, and you have Ivy-level credentials, then you might want to take a trip to see that college in person. That means you need to sign up for an official tour so the college has a record of your interest. Do not just stroll around the campus on your own.

Showing demonstrated interest is especially important if you live near campus (anything under a four-hour drive). If you reside in Chicago and you've never visited Northwestern, then they might not consider your interest genuine.

If timing or finances prevent you from visiting your top college(s), do not despair, but make sure that you articulate somewhere in your application that your aim is true.

Demonstrating How Difficult It Is to Explain Demonstrated Interest

Demonstrated interest is a nightmare to explain. Not every college uses it, and even those that do, use it in different ways. "It depends" is perhaps never more apt than when it comes to the question of demonstrated interest. And families tend to go nutty about it.

Students and parents think colleges are judgmental and jealous. They tend to believe that colleges really ought to know and like the student for them to be admitted. The notion that colleges like to see students who demonstrate interest (which can be accomplished in a variety of ways: campus visit, meeting the admissions officer during a high school visit, having an optional interview, etc.) validates this oft-inflated concern.

When I was a rep attending college fairs, I remember multiple students coming to my table and whispering to me, "I'm *very* interested." And that was that. As if whispering a coded message was somehow supposed to make me swoon and admit them. That is what drives people crazy about the very existence of demonstrated interest: Colleges want to accept students with a genuine interest in the institution, but if students (and college counselors) know that it's a weighted part of the admissions consideration, then demonstrated interest comes across as artificial.

You can have your college counselor ask the colleges if they track demonstrated interest. Some schools even come right out and say so on their website. You can also research how much importance a college places on demonstrated interest by looking up the information in the school's **Common Data Set**. Even with all this information hiding in plain sight, my intrepid school newspaper reporters once called up dozens of schools to verify their stance on demonstrated interest, and it turned out that some admissions officers said that their view of demonstrated interest was different than their posted policy.

Manic Pixie Dream Schools

In 2007, film critic Nathan Rabin coined the term Manic Pixie Dream Girl to describe Kirsten Dunst's character in the romantic tragicomedy *Elizabethtown*. Similar to Natalie Portman in *Garden State,* Kate Hudson in *Almost Famous,* and Zooey Deschanel in both *Yes Man* and *(500) Days of Summer*, the Manic Pixie Dream Girl is characterized as "that bubbly [...] creature that exists solely in the fevered imaginations of sensitive writer-directors to teach broodingly soulful young men to embrace life and its infinite mysteries and adventures."

More recently, films have begun featuring Manic Pixie Dream Boys such as Skylar Astin in *Pitch Perfect* and Ansel Elgort in *The Fault in Our Stars*. Freelance writer Anna Breslaw claims these young men are "determined to make your life magical, whether you want it or not."

Regardless of gender, these characters function to coax moody and sullen protagonists out of their gloom in order to embrace the possibilities of life. In a way, the Manic Pixie is an archetype that many colleges embrace. Just look at some college brochures and pamphlets:

> Vanderbilt: *Dream on*
>
> University of Chicago: *Transform yourself and the world*
>
> Sewanee: *You're Going to Find Out Just How Great You Are*

The Manic Pixie Dream College exists exclusively, selflessly, to benefit the student and teach important life lessons, never asking for anything in return (other than your application and tuition, of course).

In *(500) Days of Summer*, Tom (played by Joseph Gordon Levitt) explains why he loves Summer, and he sounds just like a college brochure: "I love how she makes me feel, like anything's possible, or like life is worth it."

Colleges want you to feel the same way.

Everyone's Gone to the Movies

There is a reason why the entertainment industry loves making movies and TV shows about high school—almost everybody went to high school (or will get there soon enough). While some students go willingly and others are compelled to attend, for most people high school is a universal experience.

College is a different story. Within the last decade, only about one-third of Americans have at least a bachelor's degree, while 84 percent have graduated high school. So if you make a movie about high school, you have a built-in audience. Make a film about college, and you've significantly reduced your target audience. It's the same reason Hollywood wants its potential blockbusters rated PG-13 (even in absurd cases like *Suicide Squad*), because R-rated films restrict box office potential.

Through the years, there have been some seminal (and quite a few forgettable) movies that dealt with the college admissions process. For better or (mostly) for worse, these movies are rife with misinformation about how colleges work. If all you did to prepare for college is watch these movies, you would have a pretty warped view of reality.

In the movies, college looks like a lot of fun, but in the real world, trying to get into college is a different story. Even today, most people's image of college fraternity life is based on National Lampoon's *Animal House*, a movie released in 1978 and set in 1962!

GET REAL: Many of the most common misconceptions and myths about the admissions process come from movies. Whenever I see a film that deals with getting into college, I know it's going to worry students and parents.

College Movie Sins

Movies are make-believe. And movies about getting into college are almost always devoid of any real usefulness in understanding the college process. Here are a few notable examples:

Risky Business (1983): Tom Cruise plays Joel Goodson (he's a good son, get it?), a straight-arrow high school senior who gets involved with call girls and Guido the Killer Pimp when his parents go out of town, all while Joel tries desperately to keep his eye on the prize: Princeton. And if things go badly, then it "looks like University of Illinois."

Joel's SAT scores are reportedly 597 Math and 560 Verbal (of course, real SAT scores are only given in multiples of 10). He has a 3.14 GPA and is ranked No. 52 in his class, which puts him roughly in the 84th percentile (about 615 students) in his suburban Chicago school. His top extracurricular activities are JV tennis and Recording Secretary of the Spanish Club.

Even with a glowing recommendation from the interviewer (who *really* enjoys meeting some of Joel's lady friends), there is no way Joel is getting into Princeton, even back in 1983.

FUN FACT: Tom Cruise never went to college.

Orange County (2002): Shaun, played by Colin Hanks, is a brilliant student and gifted writer living in southern California who dreams of attending Stanford.

Lily Tomlin portrays the worst college counselor in the universe. She convinces Shaun that he should only apply to Stanford (because he's a "shoo-in"), but he is denied because she mixes up his transcript with one from an idiotic classmate, who predictably gets admitted.

Instead of just contacting Stanford to explain the error, Shaun concludes that his only recourse is to persuade his wealthy, estranged father to donate a bunch of money to Stanford, which his dad refuses to do.

In the real world, anyone could have picked up the phone and straightened out the transcript snafu, but then there would have been no movie.

FUN FACT: Inept English teacher Mr. Burke (Mike White) thinks William Shakespeare wrote plays that were later adapted into *Hamlet*, *West Side Story*, *The Talented Mr. Ripley*, *Waterworld*, and *Gladiator*.

Legally Blonde (2001): Even in the movie universe, getting into Harvard Law School just to show a guy that you can be taken seriously is a pretty serious leap of faith. Although she is a Hawaiian Tropic Girl and president of her sorority, it strains the boundaries of credulity that Elle Woods (Reese Witherspoon) could get into Harvard Law. For all the absurdity of the premise, Witherspoon gives a winning performance and isn't a total ditz (she does have a 4.0 as an undergrad, buckles down to prep for the LSAT, and makes a killer admissions video in a hot tub).

FUN FACT: *Love Story* (1970) was the last movie allowed to film on the Harvard campus.

Admission (2013): A Princeton admissions officer (Tina Fey) breaks all the rules regarding minimal standards ("this is the worst transcript I've ever seen") because she is convinced that an applicant is her long-lost son whom she gave up for adoption. A montage of applicants showing off their skills/flaws is the highlight of an otherwise ho-hum film.

FUN FACT: One of my former students, Kat Edmonson, sings the song "Lucky," which plays during a Tina Fey montage in the middle of the film—and her character's name is Portia Nathan!

Back to School (1986): This Rodney Dangerfield comedy showed us that if you donate enough money to endow the Thornton Mellon School of Business, you can go to Grand Lakes University with your son and still have NCAA eligibility left to win the big diving meet by performing the legendary Triple Lindy. And you can afford to pay Kurt Vonnegut to ghostwrite your English paper on Kurt Vonnegut.

Animal House (1978): We learned all about double-secret probation, that "knowledge is good," and being fat, drunk, and stupid is no way to go through life.

FUN FACT: The scenes at Faber College (a stand-in for Dartmouth) were actually filmed at the University of Oregon.

Pitch Perfect (2012), **Pitch Perfect 2** (2015) & **Pitch Perfect 3** (2017): This film franchise is responsible for every college now having at least three acapella groups. And at no point do they actually show any character in a college classroom.

In a World Gone Mad...

Consider the language that movie trailers use, then read over some college paraphernalia. Notice any similarities? Maybe it's the bold language or specific adjectives, but every word is chosen to elicit a reaction.

Colleges have myriad ways to influence students to apply: advertising, mailers, college fairs, and high school visits.

Students need to be just as deliberate in marketing themselves.

ALPHABET SOUP

The Acronymization of Higher Education

CHAPTER 6

When I think back on all the crap I learned in high school,
It's a wonder I can think at all.
And though my lack of education hasn't hurt me none,
I can read the writing on the wall.

— *Paul Simon, "Kodachrome"*

T HE FIRST TIME YOU VENTURED into a Starbucks, you probably thought everyone there had invented their own language: *I'll have a grande quad nonfat one-pump no-whip mocha.*

Before long, you had mastered the lingo and could explain to the barista exactly what you wanted with a minimum of syllables: *Fat-Free Iced Caramel Macchiato, Upside Down.*

The nomenclature gets a whole lot more complicated when college admissions comes into play, but knowing the terminology is helpful, especially if you are trying to make sense of all the data and shorthand used by the insiders.

This chapter serves as a primer for the acronyms, initialisms, and jargon that college insiders like to use and explains what it all means.

EA vs. ED

To borrow a well-worn *Lord of the Rings* meme: One Does Not Simply *Apply* to College.

First, you have to decide if you will apply early. Depending on the school, you will apply EA or ED.

EA is Early Action, which is non-binding.

ED stands for Early Decision, which is binding. (Just remember that with Early Decision, Everything's Done).

A few schools offer **Restrictive Early Action**, which limits the number of other colleges where a student may apply. Even if students are accepted REA, they are not required to accept the offer and have until May 1 to decide, just like students who are accepted Regular Decision. Schools with REA include Boston College, Notre Dame, Stanford and many of the Ivy League schools. For the purpose of our discussion, EA and REA will be synonymous.

Colleges typically notify both EA and ED students no later than mid-December, which leaves some (but not a lot of) time for seniors to fill out more applications by the Regular Decision deadline in January.

In the old days (like 2014), things were fairly simple for students applying early. If they knew exactly which school they wanted to attend, and they were not too worried about cost, then applying Early Decision was a no-brainer. If they got in, great! That meant they were done and no longer had to bother filling out any more applications. And if students got in Early Action, they *could* be done, or they could fill out a few more applications just to see where else they get in. Maybe the Early Action college didn't offer as much financial aid they were expecting, or maybe they applied EA to a school *near* the top of their list but, since they got in, they decide to take a chance and try for some reach schools, too.

GET REAL: Many elite colleges accept between 35 to 55 percent of their students from the much smaller early applicant pool. So if you hear that a college is accepting only 8 percent of its applicants, it might actually be closer to 18 percent for Early Decision and only 6 percent for Regular Decision.

Some clear differences between Early Decision acceptance rates and Regular Decision for the 2014-2015 admission cycle were found at the following schools. The first line shows the percentage of applicants accepted Early Decision and the corresponding percentage of the freshman class filled during this round. The second line shows the percentage of Regular Decision applicants accepted and the remaining percentage of the freshman class filled. For all of these colleges, early applicants were roughly three times as likely to get accepted during the early admissions cycle than students who applied regular.

Amherst
Early: 35.4% accepted (36% of class)
Regular: 12.5% accepted (64% of class)

Brown
Early: 18.5% accepted (36.6% of class)
Regular: 7.6% accepted (63.4% of class)

Claremont-McKenna
Early: 26.4% accepted (54.4% of class)
Regular: 8.8% accepted (45.6% of class)

Columbia
Early: 20% accepted (43.6% of class)
Regular: 6.1% accepted (56.4% of class)

Dartmouth
Early: 28% accepted (40.9% of class)
Regular: 9.9% accepted (59.1% of class)

Duke
Early: 31% accepted (43.7% of class)
Regular: 10.8% accepted (56.3% of class)

Northwestern
Early: 35.3% accepted (45.3% of class)
Regular: 11.2% accepted (54.7% of class)

UPenn
Early: 25.3% accepted (53.6% of class)
Regular: 7.9% accepted (46.4% of class)

To make matters more complex, many colleges have a deadline in between the November 1 deadline for EA/ED and the Regular Decision deadline of January 1. These dates are approximate. Some schools have deadlines as early as October 15, and some Regular Decision deadlines can be as late as February. Case in point: the University of

"When someone loves a college very, very much, they apply Early Decision."

Richmond has its Richmond Scholars deadline on December 1. Only students who apply by then can receive merit awards ranging from one-third tuition to full tuition, plus room and board. So, if you are denied or waitlisted by your early school, you will miss the Richmond deadline for merit aid. Sure, you can still apply to Richmond as a Regular Decision applicant, but it reduces your financial flexibility.

Dozens of selective colleges also offer a second round of early admissions, known as Early Decision II. The deadline for these schools is usually January 1. These binding applications are utilized by students who didn't get into their EDI school or for students who weren't prepared to choose a school by the EDI deadline.

Most students do not have the luxury to apply early to just one school and then wait until December to decide where else to apply, which negates one of the main incentives for applying early in the first place.

You will want to strategize your early application(s) carefully with your college counselor. Most early plans (especially ED) *do* give an edge to the applicants who pursue them. While colleges may insist that there is no advantage, the data suggests otherwise. Moreover, even when others claim that "early doesn't help you" at a given college, there is still the reality that when you apply early, the admissions officer knows that you are keen enough on attending that college to get your application in, and as an added bonus, there are fewer students competing in the pool.

In the fall of 2015, American University in Washington, DC, accepted 87.2 percent of early applicants—compared to 32.4 percent of those who applied regular decision (the widest margin of any college). Leave it to Georgetown University to buck the trend—they admitted just 13.3 percent of early applicants and 19.4 percent of those who applied regular decision—but this is hardly the norm.

SUBURBAN LEGEND: Does the Early Bird Really Get the Worm?

Students and schools often misinterpret admissions results during different periods of evaluation. They do this because all they see is that, of the six students from their school who are so "bright and wonderful," none of them got in during an early round. And when some students from their school do get in Regular Decision, then that must be the reason! All told, this is a pretty naïve quest for the secret handshake.

Be sure to listen to the advice given by your college counselor when it comes to early plans. Many times a counselor (who is merely acting as the messenger about the reality of highly selective admissions) is seen by the family as "not supporting his (read: *our*) aspirations." That is not the case at all, but there is a reason we worry about the B- student thinking that Yale is possible.

Our goal is to advise, and as good as we are at predicting admission, we do not have the gift of prophecy. We are a lot like meteorologists—we have vast experience and data, but we are never right 100 percent of the time.

Most admissions decisions do not shock me, but when I do get a surprise, it's usually the good kind ("You got in *where*!?"). Every year at least one student will walk into my office grinning like the Cheshire Cat to gleefully announce that they got into a college that I considered a reach. Of course, I want all my students to get in everywhere because that makes them happy and, more importantly, mom is happy. To quote Walter White: "Everybody wins."

PRO TIP: Applying to college is not a raffle. Do not pick an ED or EA school on a whim.

Every year there are students who do not want to apply anywhere early, even under non-binding Early Action. This is a head-scratcher and really puts them at a disadvantage. College counselors are trying to help students find a higher education home. If there are some options for enrollment early on in the process, then it makes the college counselor's job easier *and* allows the student to explore institutions where they are admitted. Most of the students who stomp their feet about not applying early are usually doing so out of some sort of misguided principle.

GET REAL: Early admission options almost always offer an advantage strategically. Even if they do not offer a boost to admissibility, they can help with the long-term decision of where to enroll by receiving the news sooner.

Bloom Where You Are Planted: How Much Does Your High School Matter?

Almost every institution of higher learning in the United States uses a 4.0 grading scale with A's, B's, C's, D's, and F's.

But when it comes to high schools, there is a seemingly endless array of grading scales, curricula (courses and overarching philosophy), and policies—all of which are the product of the school mission statement, state or school district laws, and/or parental expectations.

Consequently, these differences make several popular admissions questions tricky to answer because one cannot realistically assess any two seemingly identical high schools the same way. An admissions office is going to consider a variety of factors regarding each high school *before* they evaluate the applicants:

- How many graduates attend two-year and four-year colleges?
- How many students are on free or reduced lunch?
- Does the high school rank its students?
- How many AP, IB, or Honors classes are available?
- Are there policies limiting how many advanced courses a student may take?

There are a dozen questions that could be added, but the big question is: **Did this student succeed within the context of their high school?** In other words: **Did this student bloom where she was planted?**

What may come as a surprise is that one's GPA, in and of itself, is often a meaningless number in admissions. Asking a college, "What's the average GPA of an admitted student?" is fairly pointless because every high school has particular grading policies.

Curiously, some colleges will publish a recalculated GPA on a universal 4.0 scale. The University of Richmond once took the GPAs of all admitted students and averaged them together to show their average GPA, which they posted on their blog. The hilarious result was that the average GPA was around 25.0 because it included 100-point grading scales as well as those using a 4-point scale.

AP vs. IB vs. Honors courses

Some high schools have AP classes, some have IB, some have honors, some have a mix, and some have none of the above. It depends.

AP is the ubiquitous **Advanced Placement Program** organized by the College Board (which also administers the SAT, among other standardized tests). The philosophy of the AP program is that students take a "college level" course in their high school, which doubles as a year-long test preparation for the AP Exam in that subject during the first two weeks of May. These exams are scored on a 1-5 scale (whole numbers only) with 1 being the lowest and 5 being the highest. According to the College Board, a score of 3 or better on an AP Exam is considered "passing."

Once a student decides where they wish to enroll for college, that school might give college credit for every AP Exam that meets a minimum threshold, making early graduation possible and/or fulfilling standard curriculum requirements.

GET REAL: The academic departments within the colleges tend to determine how much college credit they will award to students based on their AP scores. Some Ultras will award credit for a score of a 5, a few will also consider a 4, but there are some non-Ultras that will give credit for a 3, so be sure to check. Some colleges limit how much AP credit they award, but even the most talented student is unlikely to hit the maximum.

Students will often enroll in AP classes because they are interested in the material, they wish to challenge themselves (an important but often misunderstood criteria in the admissions process), or they seek college credit.

IB stands for **International Baccalaureate**, and it functions much like a cousin of the AP program. IB classes are rigorous, just like the AP, and they have corresponding exams with scores ranging from 1 (lowest) to 7 (highest). Like the APs, colleges will give course credit for high scores, typically a 6 or 7 on the IB exams. Students that go the extra mile and earn the **IB Diploma** can receive additional credit hours from some colleges.

Does This Curriculum Make Me Look Smart?

Attend any college information session and inevitably someone in the audience (most likely a parent) will ask about high school curriculum: *Do you like to see AP, IB or Honors courses?*

The stock answer is that if those courses are available, then admissions officers are going to expect students to avail themselves of some challenging classes—but not necessarily *all* of them.

The follow-up question is just as predictable: *Is it better to get an A in the regular class or a B in the AP/IB/Honors course?*

The snarky admissions office answer is just as predictable: *It's better to get an A in the advanced course.*

So what's a student to do?

Take comfort in knowing that the admissions office is going to look at the curriculum you were offered, what the policies were for enrolling in it (limits on number of APs a student may pursue, etc.), and how you challenged yourself.

Colleges will not hold it against you if you are not an all-star hockey player because you grew up in Louisiana, and they will not ding you if you took as many honors classes as you could without negatively impacting your health.

SUBURBAN LEGEND: Easy Street

The twisted logic goes something like this: Take the least rigorous classes to get the highest GPA!

There are some families in this land of rugged individuals who think that taking the path of least resistance is a bold, innovative approach that will surely impress the admissions office. After all, how will they know if the school offers tougher classes? It is an absolute wonder that people do not comprehend why this strategy is unlikely to make a good impression.

Even the Ultras do not *require* taking every rigorous course, although most admitted students do have challenging course loads. **The best advice is to take as rigorous a curriculum as you can reasonably, sanely, and healthily handle that does not overwhelm you.** If you have several APs, but you are getting below a B in any course, your rigor is perhaps too much. So, humanities students should avail themselves of more rigor in those areas, whereas students entering STEM fields should pursue rigor in those courses.

GET REAL: Some students are worried about "not having taken a given course," thus dooming their chances of admission. This is almost always much ado about very little. Yes, business programs want to see strong math courses, and engineering programs typically want to see Physics and Calculus on the transcript, but I once had a student worried sick that his chances of majoring in theater would be soured because there was rumor that his college of choice "really wanted to see Physics on the transcript." Um, no. Pursue the courses and rigor that most closely align with what you might want to study. Most students do that organically anyway.

Secondary Testing: AP, IB, & SAT Subject Test Scores

Primary testing consists of the ACT or SAT exams. **Secondary testing** consists of AP, IB, and SAT Subject Test Scores. Colleges cannot require AP or IB scores because not every high school student can avail themselves of those course offerings and the corresponding tests. Some colleges require SAT Subject Tests (although many are moving away from these requirements) or will accept a combination of those test scores *in lieu of* a primary SAT or ACT score.

GET REAL: One of the things that students fret about is what a "low" secondary test score will do to the competitiveness of their application. These low scores are often in the eye of the beholder and are often quite competitive. Their concern might be due to the fact that SAT Subject Tests are listed by percentile. Even students who score a perfect 800 could be in the 88th percentile (which means 12 percent of all students scored an 800); however, admissions officers do not see or care about percentiles. Even one truly low score will usually be viewed as an outlier and is not a cause for concern.

Strong secondary testing ultimately affects the student's overall **Academic Rating**, which is easily the most important metric in admissions evaluations. Although it is calculated differently at each institution, **the Academic Rating is a function of grades, curriculum, test scores, and grade trends.** When a student provides strong secondary testing, it can bump up the overall rating.

A's vs. B's

On the surface, this seems like a moot point—an A is better than a B. Or is it? Remember, colleges want students to take the most rigorous courses possible, so there is considerable pressure for students to challenge themselves with the toughest schedule. But what happens if grades suffer as a result of taking too many hard classes—or just that one class really kicks your butt? How much lower can the grades get before the challenging schedule hurts the student's admissibility?

Let's consider the final grades from three applicants from different high schools.

Sabrina: 93 in Chemistry (Regular Level)
Kelly: 88 in Chemistry (Honors)
Kris: 83 in AP Chemistry

Now look at their AP Chemistry test scores (taken at the end of junior year)
Sabrina: 2
Kelly: 4
Kris: 5

How would an admissions officer evaluate these three students? Get out your gray paint because it's not black-and-white, and there is no clear answer.

Sabrina has the best grade but the lowest AP score. Kris is just the opposite. And Kelly is in the middle. Perhaps Kris's AP Chemistry teacher is the toughest yet prepared her the best for the exam since she got a 5. Kelly's quite respectable 88 in Honors Chemistry correlates nicely with a 4 on the exam. Sabrina's 2 will not get her college credit anywhere, but her 93 average looks nice. Perhaps Sabrina should have enrolled in Honors Chemistry, which would have prepared her better for the AP.

It depends, it depends, and it depends.

Kelly probably has the better overall stats since she has a solid grade in a rigorous course and even challenged herself to take the AP exam, ultimately earning a 4, which will likely get her college credit. Does that mean Kelly will always be the most competitive? That's to be argued in committee.

Where Everyone's GPA is Above Average

Grade Point Average is the number that makes most parents and students crazy.

Grades are certainly important, but the level of angst over GPA has a corrosive trickle-down effect that damages a student's relationship with both parents and teachers.

In Season 3 of *Glee*, there was an entire episode regarding parental fixation on grades. Dubbed "The Asian F," the episode centers on Mike Chang, who makes an A- on a chemistry exam. After receiving such an unacceptable grade, Mike's father wants him drug tested every day and insists that he quit the Glee Club and break up with his girlfriend because they are distractions to his goal of becoming a doctor. This cultural stereotype is a gross misrepresentation—all students who aspire to the Ultras feel the pressure to make stellar grades. One of my students lamented, "My dad thinks anything below a 96 isn't a real A."

We laugh because it's funny. We cry a little on the inside because we know it's true.

It's Not About the Grade...

As a teacher, whenever I get an email or phone call from a parent requesting a conference, it invariably includes the caveat: *It's not about the grade.*

This is a bald-faced lie.

If a conversation begins, "I don't mean any disrespect," you can be certain there will be some serious disrespecting coming up. And when parents say that it's not about the grade, well, *it's always about the grade.*

A few years ago, the parents of one of my juniors called me early in the school year to schedule a conference regarding their daughter's performance. They assured me it was not about the grade (at the first checkpoint she had an 88).

By the time mom and dad came in, I had graded a major essay and some other assignments that had raised her average significantly. When they sat down, I began by nonchalantly checking her grade, which was up to a 94. Then I told them that their daughter was one of my best students.

So, what would you like to talk about?

Whatever speech they had practiced was never delivered. Suddenly, they had nothing to say other than how much she loved the class and how proud they were of her. Our "conference" lasted all of three minutes.

Don't Be the Squeaky Wheel

Like many of you, I enjoy sampling books before I buy them, and that means going to the bookstore. One summer, while my son was out at the field warming up for a baseball game, I was killing time at a nearby Books-A-Million. I came across a college admissions book that actually advised parents and students to take an aggressive stance with teachers: "Let the teachers know that you expect an A in the class and will not tolerate anything less." The fuzzy logic they promoted is that teachers (especially those in public schools) will kowtow to families with high expectations so they do not have to deal with the aggravation that will surely result if they "give" the kid a B.

I seriously wanted to fling the book across the store in disgust, but instead I *accidentally* re-shelved the book in Science Fiction.

PRO TIP: Do not be one of those parents who constantly argues with teachers about grades. You have every right to respectfully inquire if there is a real issue, but it should be up to the students to advocate for themselves when it comes to day-to-day grading. You might think that you are helping (and you should be supportive of your kids), but you run the risk of sounding like one of those crazy soccer moms or baseball dads who think that the universe is conspiring against their child. As we will see in Chapter 9, you might need these teachers to write a letter of recommendation one day, and if you burn too many bridges, you may find that you have made it harder, not easier, for your child to get into college.

This Is Me in Grade 9

Students are often shocked to discover just how important freshman year can be. Here's a simple way to think about it: Freshman year has the greatest disparity grade-wise between the ceiling and the floor. Some kids will make straight A's at every grade level throughout high school, but there are far more low grades in ninth grade. Freshman year can be a disaster for any number of reasons, including the fact that many kids come from a wide range of middle schools that might not have adequately prepared them for high school, so it may take longer for those students to get acclimated to the rigors of high school.

A few colleges do not even take freshman year grades into account. When colleges look at grades, how students perform in 11th grade is certainly more important than how they do in ninth. But the cold, cruel GPA does not care about that. Numbers do not lie, and if you are applying to one of the Ultras or a state school that grants automatic admission based on class rank, then every 1/100th of a grade point matters.

By the time students reach senior year, there is a natural tendency for grades to rise. The good news is that many seniors can point to an upward trend in grades; the bad news is that those who stumbled out of the starting blocks are often hopelessly behind in the GPA race.

In lieu of actually making consistently good grades from eighth grade onward (Surprise! Some high schools include middle school grades in math, science, foreign language, and even debate in order to compute the GPA), there are a few shortcuts that students can take to boost their GPA—some simple, others extreme.

Pulling the Old Switcheroo

In the Houston Independent School District, in order to qualify as valedictorian or salutatorian, a student must be enrolled in the same high school since the beginning of the spring semester of their junior year. What a few families do is enroll their kids in private schools that offer an abundance of honors classes (even in courses like Dance) and then have the students transfer into a public school after two or two-and-a-half years with a GPA boost that the kids who have been in the public high school from the beginning cannot possibly match.

A less Machiavellian option is putting off required courses that have no honors component—like Health or Speech. These classes are typically taken by freshmen but can only net a 4.0 average, which actually lowers the GPA of kids applying to the Ultras or hoping to graduate in the top 10 percent. If students are willing to wait and take these classes with a bunch of freshmen during their senior year, then they can improve their GPA/class rank since high schools and college admissions typically only use 3.5 years of data.

GET REAL: Admissions officers actually do not have much use for your GPA. It's a poor academic summary. Granted, a student with, say, a 3.8 is presumably a stronger student than one with a 3.2, but the reality is that admissions officers are going to look at grades, grading scales, curricula, and so on. Thus, one's GPA, in and of itself, is not totally helpful to an admissions officer because they are much more concerned with how the GPA is calculated than the calculation itself.

We're All Number One!

Some schools and school districts have policies that each and every student who reaches a predetermined grade point average is considered a valedictorian. For instance, in 2015, there were 222 valedictorians at Dublin Jerome High School in Ohio. This is madness on multiple levels and leads admissions officers to roll their eyes in disbelief.

While this system might appear to reduce the unhealthy competition that comes from rewarding a single valedictorian and salutatorian, if there are dozens (or hundreds!) of valedictorians, the colleges will find their own way to rank these students.

PSAT vs. SAT (or ACT)

The **PSAT** (Preliminary Scholastic Aptitude Test) is administered by the College Board and takes place on a Wednesday in mid-October for high school juniors.

Sophomores (and some freshmen) take the test as well, but those scores do not count—it is merely a "Practice PSAT." Seeing how students perform on the PSAT as an underclassman can signal to a student (and school) where they stand in relation to the other students, and it can address areas of weakness where students should focus in order to prepare for the high-stakes standardized tests they will take junior and senior year.

The PSAT and SAT got revamped in 2015, leading to much confusion about how to interpret the scores based on previous years. It did not help matters that the student percentiles listed on the PSAT score sheets made it seem like everyone was in the 90th percentile.

Students should prepare themselves for a steady stream of direct mail and email coming from colleges after they take the PSAT—it begins as a trickle sophomore year and eventually becomes a deluge.

Here's the upshot of the PSAT: It matters more than the SAT or ACT—for scholarships. It does not matter much, if at all, for admission.

SUBURBAN LEGEND: Does the PSAT Get You Into College?

Let's dispel one of the most common misconceptions: **PSAT scores do not enter into the equation for college admissions**—they are more symbolic than significant. There isn't even a place on college applications to put these scores. They do, however, put you in contention for all kinds of merit-based aid.

Twenty-five years ago, a number of highly selective schools would fall all over themselves courting **National Merit Finalists** (those who finish in the top one percent in each state), but today the Ultras give no consideration (or money) to applicants just because they are National Merit Finalists.

Some opportunistic colleges, looking to increase their profile by having a large number of National Merit Finalists, have stepped up their financial investment. Here's the 2017 National Merit Finalist leaderboard:

University of Oklahoma (317)	University of Minnesota (159)
University of Chicago (259)	MIT (156)
USC (257)	Yale (156)
Harvard (219)	Northeastern (153)
Vanderbilt (219)	Texas A&M (148)
University of Florida (202)	Purdue (141)
Northwestern (200)	University of California, Berkeley (136)
Stanford (168)	University of Alabama (134)
University of Texas, Dallas (160)	Arizona State (126)

Like many other large state schools, Oklahoma puts considerable resources into Honors Colleges designed to create a small school feel in a large school environment—a problem with which the small private schools on the list do not have to contend.

For two decades, Oklahoma made a commitment to bolster its reputation with generous scholarships for National Merit Finalists, offering full tuition plus room and board, fees, and a technology stipend, but in 2018 OU scaled back its National Merit aid. Their scholarships are still substantial enough to keep them on this list, but they are not nearly enticing enough to convince as many out-of-state applicants to spend four years in Norman, Oklahoma.

An Offer He Couldn't Refuse

In 2015, Ronald Nelson, a senior at Houston High School (a public school in Germantown, Tennessee), was accepted by all eight Ivy League schools (as well as Stanford and Johns Hopkins). He turned them all down in order to attend the University of Alabama—and Crimson Tide head football coach Nick Saban had nothing to do with it. Alabama offered Nelson a full academic scholarship and the others did not. This is precisely why colleges offer scholarships.

A decade earlier, Roger Thompson, associate vice-president for enrollment management at the University of Alabama, bemoaned spending so much money to lure scholars. "I hate it," Thompson said. "You have to have X number of National Merit Scholars and all that. The rankings thing is out of the barn."

In a 2005 article in Atlantic Monthly, Thompson explained how schools like Alabama use their financial aid budget: "The National Merit kids, they're going to get a full ride. But if you're sitting at a private high school [...] where they pay twenty grand to go, we don't even bring financial-aid material. What's the point? You don't even need to talk about cost."

If you are not caught up in the name brand college experience, which will cost almost a quarter of a million dollars at most Ultras, then there are some affordable options for National Merit Finalists.

In addition to Oklahoma, Florida, and Alabama, here are some schools that offer full tuition (plus other perks like travel and technology stipends) when it comes to recruiting National Merit Finalists:

Texas A&M University	Louisiana Tech
University of Arizona	University of Mississippi
Florida International	University of Nebraska
University of Kentucky	University of Houston

Every year students turn down full-ride scholarships to exceptional schools in order to pay full price at one of the Ultras. In just the last few years, I witnessed one student pass on the prestigious Morehead Scholarship at the University of North Carolina to attend MIT, another gave up a Jefferson Scholarship at the University of Virginia after getting off the Stanford waitlist, another turned down a sizable scholarship at Duke in order to attend Princeton, and yet another turned down a full-ride at Wake Forest as soon as he got off the waitlist at Harvard. During his freshman year in Cambridge, this student asked me, "Why aren't the people here as awesome as I thought they'd be?"

ACT vs. SAT (and the Old SAT vs the New SAT)

During my freshman year in high school, I had an initial meeting with my counselor, Mr. Scott. As we plotted out my four years of study, he made the following prediction: "By the time you graduate, the ACT will be more popular than the SAT."

Mr. Scott may have been 30 years premature with his prognostication, but he was not wrong. In 2014, the ACT (with 1.85 million tests taken) overtook the SAT (1.67 million) as the standardized test of choice. In many ways, the battle over college testing supremacy is reminiscent of another war that waged during my high school years—Coke versus Pepsi.

For those of you who are not veterans of the Great Cola Wars, here is a brief summary you will not find in your history textbooks:

Pepsi and Coke were engaged in a battle royal to determine the industry leader in sugary carbonated beverages. After decades as a regional cola, Pepsi began to chip away at Coke's hegemony, buoyed by their sponsorship deals with young mega stars like Madonna and Michael Jackson. Pepsi latched onto the MTV crowd and dubbed themselves The Choice of a New Generation. They boldly asked anyone to take the Pepsi Challenge and see for themselves which cola was better.

Coke was the venerable soda institution. Sure, their once-mighty market position was eroding, but they were still the king. But then, in 1985, Coke did the unthinkable.

They introduced New Coke.

By changing the secret formula—and simultaneously ceasing production of "Old" Coke—people went nuts, resulting in mass protests and hoarding. When the dust settled, Coke brought back Old Coke, but they lost their mighty stronghold on the market, and Pepsi became a legitimate national brand.

Today, the comparison between standardized testing services and colas isn't all that different. After years of being a mostly regional test favored by schools in the northeast, the ACT established a niche outside their base as an alternative to the stodgy SAT, which had come under fire for racial and socioeconomic bias and antiquated sections that relied on obscure vocabulary words.

The SAT had their New Coke moment in 2005 when the College Board changed some types of questions (goodbye analogies), added an essay section, and changed the scoring scale from 1600 to 2400.

After a decade of losing ground to the ACT, the SAT got another overhaul in 2015 (back to the 1600-point scale!) and adopted changes that made it look more like the ACT.

And everyone lost their minds.

Education Facts

Serving Size: 1 SAT Test
Servings per container: 1 (or 2, or 3)

Minutes 225	Minutes of break 20
	% Daily Value
Reading	33%
Math	33%
Writing	33%
Year established	1926
Grading scale (no essay)	1600
Test takers (2014)	1.67 mil

Education Facts

Serving Size: 1 ACT Test
Servings per container: 1 (or 2, or 3)

Minutes 175	Minutes of break 25
	% Daily Value
Reading	25%
Math	25%
Writing	25%
Science	25%
Year established	1959
Grading scale	36
Test takers (2014)	1.85 mil

THE CHOICE OF A
NEW GENERATION

GRAPHICS BY ASHWINI BAND

Because the SAT could not guarantee getting practice materials to students and test prep companies in time, there was a mad dash by juniors to take the Old SAT in the fall of 2015 before the New SAT was instituted in 2016.

Counselors began advising families to take the ACT because they knew what they were getting. As for the SAT, most experts adopted a wait-and-see approach. And, as we noted in Chapter 4, those who went with the crowd saw the overall ACT score drop.

The ACT Essay Disaster of 2015

The ACT is far from perfect, as evidenced by its wildly inconsistent grading of the essay section. For years, two ACT graders would evaluate a student's writing, giving them a score of 1 to 6. These two scores were added together for a final score of 2 to 12. Then the ACT decided to bring the scoring scale for the essay in line with the other sections of the test, which meant a score out of 36.

And then the scores came out.

Students who scored in the 30s on the reading section somehow also received low 20s or high teens on the essay. Suddenly all those students who chose to take the ACT instead of the New SAT had a major problem.

Those families that were savvy enough paid $50 to have the essays re-scored by the ACT, and what do you think happened? Miraculously, many of those same essays received scores 2 to 10 points higher (the ACT also refunded the regrading fee if the scores went up by at least two points).

Unsurprisingly, in June 2016, the ACT announced they would return to the old 2-12 essay scoring scale.

While the ACT held the top spot for many years, the SAT finally re-established itself as the leader in the standardized testing world in 2018 (2.1 million vs. 1.91 million), but clearly the ACT is here to stay.

Mr. Scott would be pleased.

SUBURBAN LEGEND: Timing Isn't Everything

Here's one of the most resilient fallacies around: People are convinced that there are certain times of the year when it is easier to get a good score on the ACT or SAT.

I heard this rumor back in 2015 when one of my newspaper editors, a junior, informed me that he couldn't attend our national journalism convention because he had to stay home to take the November SAT.

I asked him why he didn't just sign up for the SAT in October, December, or January, and he told me that his mother had heard that the November test was "easier" because allegedly fewer of the really smart kids took the test that month, so he would get a better score.

All criticisms of the College Board aside, standardized tests would not be worth anything as a measuring device for students if they were not...oh, what's the word? Standardized! It does not matter when or where you take the test; there is a process in place to ensure comparable scores.

There is no easier time to take the SAT or ACT.

There are certainly times when taking a standardized test would be *better for you*, so if you do not want to take the December test because it takes place during the football playoffs or the June test because it falls during Ramadan, then you need to choose your test dates in advance.

Sometimes an "easy" test is a bad thing.

Students who were retaking the SAT exam in June of 2018 got quite a surprise when the scores came out. Many students received lower scores even though they answered fewer questions incorrectly than they had on a previous version of the test.

While there is no easier time to take the SAT, there are occasionally easier tests. Responding to the outcry from students for the exam to be rescored, The College Board issued a statement: "We want to assure you that our scores are accurate. While we plan for consistency across administrations, on occasion there are some tests that can be easier or more difficult than usual."

The College Board uses a statistical process called "equating," which ensures that a score taken for a test on one date is equivalent to a score from another, so a single wrong answer on one exam might be worth two or three wrong answers on a different test.

Students who were hoping that the June 2018 exam would improve their scores were faced with the dilemma of sticking with their previous high score or signing up for the next exam in late August and hoping to fare better.

The Electric Kool-Aid ACT Test

Here are a few basics for taking standardized tests:

Take the test twice. Three times, max. The Law of Diminishing Returns will kick in if you try it more than thrice. According to the ACT, the majority of 2016 graduates who took the test (59 percent) only took it once.

Colleges vary as to which scores they want to see—if any.

Some schools want to see all your scores, no matter how many times you take the test. In 2016, UPenn abruptly reversed its policy that required students to submit all scores: ACT, SAT, and SAT Subject Tests. Stanford and Georgetown are notable holdouts that mandate submitting all SAT or ACT scores, and Georgetown goes one step further by requiring all Subject Tests be submitted as well (Stanford deems subject tests as *recommended*, not *required*).

Many universities will allow students to **superscore** (also known as **Score Choice**), which utilizes the best sections from each time a student takes the test; however, students could not combine sections from the Old SAT with the New SAT.

You are welcome to take both the SAT and ACT, especially if you take one and you do not score as well as you thought you would perform, but do not take both the SAT and ACT multiple times—that would be a waste of both time and money.

If a college requires one or two SAT Subject Tests and allows for selective submission of scores, you could take two or three tests and drop one if it is too low.

And speaking of those pesky SAT Subject Tests (once called the SAT II), a growing number of colleges, including UPenn, now state that they are *recommended* but not *required*. This trend allows students to take the subject tests but only report them to colleges if they help.

PRO TIP: Sign up for the ACT or SAT well in advance. Students do better on assessments when they are in a familiar setting, so do not risk signing up late and having to take the test at an unfamiliar place—or getting shut out completely.

GPA vs. Standardized Scores

According to the College Board, the average GPA for high school seniors went from 2.64 in 1996 to 2.90 in 2006—even though SAT scores remained basically flat. The ACT also released a longitudinal study (from 1991 to 2003) that showed grade inflation of .25 points (on a 4.0 scale), or roughly a 6.25 percent increase.

When the difference between college acceptance and denial can be micro-fractions of grade points, the issue of grade inflation will not go away.

On the one hand, the data suggests that GPA alone might not be the best way to differentiate students, but the alternative is relying even more on standardized test scores, which have some fundamental flaws beyond favoring wealthier students.

Here is where the rubber meets the road: If grades do not differentiate students, and if high schools continue to do silly things like naming 222 kids valedictorian because they all have a GPA over 4.1, then they are abdicating power to the standardized tests (which students loathe) while simultaneously reinforcing a system that benefits those who can most afford test prep services and private tutoring.

Smaller colleges can look past class rank in order to view applications holistically, but at some point all colleges need to decide how they will evaluate applicants.

Voodoo Economics

Do not get us started on the false sense of superiority that comes from 43 percent of students making an A in a course. Even little Maggie Simpson learned that "A is A" during her short stint at the Ayn Rand School for Tots.

Some brave colleges have tried to stem the tide of grade inflation, most notably Princeton, which created a policy in 2004 to deflate grades (a professor could issue an A to no more than 35 percent of students in a course), but after complaints from students and faculty that these lower grades were negatively impacting the ability of students to gain entrance to the best graduate schools or land prestigious jobs, the policy was voted down in 2014.

It is worth noting that since Princeton's decision to confront grade inflation that no other elite schools have followed suit. It is also reasonable to conclude that by limiting the number of A's, there were probably quite a few high school students who eschewed applying to Princeton.

The data from the NACAC State of College Admission Report shows that the importance of class rank as a metric in admissions has been on a slow, steady decline. In 1993, more than 40 percent of admissions counselors viewed class rank as "considerably important." By 2006, roughly 23 percent of colleges deemed that class rank was of considerable importance, and that figure dropped to just 14 percent in 2014.

To Rank or Not to Rank

You might think that something as simple as grade point average would be standardized.

But if you have a child in high school, then you probably know by now that computing a student's GPA requires an advanced mathematics degree.

First, there is the matter of what kind of scale to use:

- The traditional 4-point scale
- A weighted 5-point scale that takes into account bonus points for AP and Honors coursework
- A 10-point scale that takes a student's grade and simply puts a decimal point in (thus a 95 in a course equals a 9.5 GPA)
- A 7-point scale because, at this point, who cares?

Even on the familiar, unweighted 4-point scale, you might assume that each letter grade equals one grade point (A=4, B=3, C=2, D=1, F=0) but that would require a reminder of why we should never *assume*.

When my kids applied to college, their school computed the **Weighted GPA**, but many colleges want to know the **Unweighted GPA**, which we had to figure out.

And if you think the Houston Independent School District does things logically, here's how they compute Unweighted GPA:

$$90-100 = 4.0$$
$$80-89 = 3.0$$
$$75-79 = 2.0$$
$$70-74 = 1.0$$
$$<70 = \text{Failing}$$

Does this make any sense? Absolutely not.

Do schools and school districts mess around with formulas for capricious reasons? All the time.

While some schools and districts have abandoned listing class rank, others have developed byzantine formulas to determine theirs.

Colleges are left to make educated guesses regarding probable class rank or they must re-calibrate a school's formula and ranking system to determine where a student truly stands.

In-State vs. Out-of-State (How to Tame 'Bright Flight')

I once got a call from a frantic mother: "We read on the University of California system's website that they favor applicants from California! Is that true?!"

Um, yes.

With the University of Any State, the name of the institution is just that—an institution, just like the post office. Public universities and colleges are created and maintained by the state government to keep their students educated and the economy humming. Meanwhile, out-of-state applicants will undoubtedly complain about the state laws that require a vast majority of students to come from the home state.

Some flagship universities do struggle to retain in-state students, like the University of Vermont, where 80 percent of students enrolled for the class of 2019 were *not* locals.

On the other end of the spectrum, for years the University of California system had come under fire for taking too many out-of-state and international students at the expense of more qualified Californians. A state audit released in March 2016 confirmed that the UC system was rejecting in-state students, especially minorities, in favor of less qualified out-of-state applicants. By July 2016, the University of California announced they had increased admissions offers to in-state students by more than 15 percent while also reducing acceptances from international students at their Berkeley and San Diego campuses.

State laws make sense when you consider the *raison d'être* of these institutions.

State legislatures love to give their in-state students "hope" (scholarships). Several states became concerned that too many of their students were graduating from high school and then leaving the state to attend college elsewhere, often not returning to their home state. It's a phenomenon known as **bright flight**.

In a controversial move, several states took money from their lottery fund and gave promising students a scholarship that could be used at any institution (often public or private) within the state. This policy has been critiqued for taking money from the lottery and giving it to future college students, many of whom do not need the financial assistance as much as their low-income classmates.

In 2013, there were 12 states, along with Washington D.C., that provided more merit aid than need-based aid to their in-state high school graduates (19 states reduced *all* financial aid from 2008 to 2013). The increase in these scholarships helped stem the tide of bright flight.

PRO TIP: Most states impose a January 1 deadline for their in-state aid (need-based and merit), so be sure to apply early. In many states, the number of eligible students far exceeds the budget, which often runs out early. In Florida, almost half the eligible low-income students were turned away in 2015.

The idea sounds rational, especially for government officials: keep the best and brightest students in the state, and then those college graduates might begin their careers in-state, which is good for local economy.

The University of Georgia's academic reputation and application numbers have gone up since the state eliminated all its need-based tuition aid in 2012 in favor of HOPE (Helping Outstanding Pupils Educationally!) scholarships. Still, critics correctly point out that these HOPE scholarships often redistribute need-based scholarship funds that could assist poorer students.

The essential question remains: How can a state prevent its best and brightest students from leaving while also providing an affordable, quality education for low-income students who are less likely to leave home?

FUN FACT: Missouri actually refers to their in-state merit scholarship program as the Bright Flight Program!

Class Rank vs. Holistic Review

On June 23, 2016, the United States Supreme Court upheld a lower court decision that the University of Texas at Austin correctly applied their race-sensitive admissions policy, known as the "Top 10 Percent Rule."

The plaintiff, Abigail Fisher, applied to UT in 2008 and was denied admission. At the time, the flagship school of Texas accepted the top 10 percent of students in every high school class in the state, and approximately 81 percent of the 2008 freshman class were admitted using this plan. Fisher claimed she was discriminated against because she was white.

The UT admissions policy has created some strange bedfellows. High schools in urban areas and small towns love the policy, but the suburban schools hate it.

Regardless of where you stand on the UT policy specifically, or affirmative action in general, you need to know how admissions decisions are made and how that impacts what you do in high school.

In states like Texas, whose public universities have a system for admitting students, class rank is essential, so public schools rank students at the end of junior year and again after the first semester of their senior year. This policy is great if you want to attend the University of Texas and your class rank falls in the specified percentile. The "10 Percent Rule" is currently down to 6 percent for UT. So, if you are in a class of 550 students and are ranked No. 30, you will get into UT—*and* you satisfy a key admissions metric if you want to attend out-of-state schools.

But what if you attend a small, elite private school that issues class rank? If you have a graduating class of 100 students, and you are No. 30, then you are not close to the top 10 percent (you are not even in the top quartile). Still, if your high school is super elite and you have dozens of National Merit Finalist classmates, then fear not, a selective college (including UT) will still probably take you.

Exact class rank can work against kids in public schools who fall outside the top 10 percent and want to apply to a selective school. If a high school does not rank its students, then the colleges must look at other criteria. Simply put, if your high school does not rank you, even though you are outside the top 10 percent, then the college cannot rule against you on the basis of class rank.

AP Exams vs. Standardized Tests

In 2014, FairTest used data from the College Board and demonstrated that family income has a direct correlation to SAT scores. **For every $20,000 in family income, there is an increase in test scores**—and it's incremental across the board. Thus, many admissions officers are giving more weight to AP tests which, like the SAT, are administered by the College Board.

One advantage of the AP tests is that they measure what a student has learned in a specific course, so many school districts are encouraging schools to offer more AP classes. The logic seems sound enough—by offering more AP classes, the students will look like they are taking a more challenging course load. Unfortunately, too often students make fantastic grades in AP courses despite learning little of the content, and they wind up failing the end-of-course AP exams (defined as making a 1 or 2 on the AP).

When Terry Grier became superintendent of the Houston Independent School District in 2009, one of his progressive (and expensive) measures was to have every high school campus offer at least 15 Advanced Placement classes, and the district would even pay for the students to sit for the AP exams. But in 2012, when the district compared the grades made by students in the AP classes to their performance on the corresponding AP exams, the results were rather dreadful.

For all students making an A in an AP class, the most common grade on the corresponding exam was a 1, the lowest score possible (typically representing the bottom 10 percent of the testing pool). A-level students *did* score slightly more 5's and 4's than 3's and 2's, but all the scores other than 1 were fairly evenly distributed.

As bad as that was, the B students fared even worse. Of the 7,511 grades in the B-range, 4,091 of those students recorded a 1 on the AP. That means over half the B students in HISD scored in the bottom 10 percent of their Advanced Placement tests! Rather than looking like a bell curve, the HISD charts for B through D students look like a really steep slide—lots of 1's and virtually no 5's.

When there is a massive disconnect between classroom grades and AP scores, the colleges will notice, and it will certainly have a negative impact on the school profile.

In a perfect world, students who score a 4 or 5 on an AP test should make an A or B in the course, so **the high schools that manage to foster this kind of predictability between grades and AP scores will ultimately have a more favorable school profile.**

The number of students taking AP exams continues to rise (participation has doubled in the last 10 years) because parents push students to take the exams, even though 60 percent of their teachers report that those kids do not belong in the classes.

Proponents of expanding AP programs insist that even if students fail the AP exams, they will reap the rewards of learning what college-level work is like. Furthermore, they argue that students will benefit from being around smarter classmates and better teachers—the whole "a rising tide raises all ships" argument—except that the research, primarily from *AP: A Critical Examination of the Advanced Placement Test* (2010), refutes that claim. The research indicates that students who fail an AP exam do not fare any better in college courses than students who did not take an AP course.

In the end, whether you're hung up on A's and B's or agonizing over SAT's, knowing the admissions alphabet can help you along the way.

HOW TO CONVINCE A COMMITTEE THAT YOUR ESSAY WASN'T WRITTEN BY ONE

CHAPTER 7

I just can't find the time to write my mind
The way I want it to read.

— *Wilco, "Box Full of Letters"*

A T A YALE INFORMATION SESSION in the fall of 2013, an admissions officer had just finished her presentation to a room full of eager families and opened the floor to questions.

Students and parents asked a series of rather mundane questions until one mother got her chance to speak: "My son is a great kid, but he doesn't work in a lab searching for the cure for cancer. He's just a great kid. He works a regular job. He has friends. He's a great kid. He makes great grades, but he's not a minority and doesn't have any huge obstacle that he's overcome—he's just a great kid."

Finally she got to her question: "Does Yale accept average great kids?"

As cringe-inducing as her spiel was, this mother hit upon the suspicion that Yale and her Ivy cohorts only take the most exceptional kids because there is no room for generic greatness (applicants with solid attributes but nothing that stands out are sometimes dubbed **standard strong** in admissions). Fortunately, this great kid was not at the information session to hear his mother extol his unremarkable greatness.

What I wanted to tell this exasperated parent is that there is a way to tell the colleges exactly who you are and why they would be lucky to have you—the college essay.

The essay is the most feared part of the entire application process, and some students are so hesitant to write an essay that they will actively avoid schools that require anything more than the Common App essay, if that.

The Essay-less Application

The essay is so intimidating that some colleges lure students to apply by promising that they do not have to write an essay at all. These aren't the Ultras, mind you, but colleges have figured out that the simplest way to increase the number of applicants is to decrease the amount of writing.

Colby College in Maine dropped its supplemental essay in 2014, choosing to go with just the required personal essay on the Common App, and their application rate soared 47 percent. That same year, Swarthmore College dropped one essay and shortened another to just 250 words—applications went up 42 percent.

Some schools allow students to submit "video essays." Goucher College in northern Baltimore and Tufts have been at the vanguard of accepting these two-minute videos in order to appeal to creative extroverts.

When my older son made his first college list, he included schools with strong petroleum engineering programs, which included the Colorado School of Mines. He even designated Mines as a school that would receive his SAT scores from the College Board. Ultimately, Zach got in early to several of his top schools, so it was no longer necessary to spend another $75 to apply at Mines.

In mid-December, Zach got an email from Mines that said they would waive the application fee *and* the required essay if he would just complete a brief "priority" application. Full disclosure: Zach was a National Merit Finalist, so it's possible they didn't extend this offer to everyone, but it was certainly an enticement. He applied to Mines and was quickly accepted. Ultimately the financial aid package wasn't as strong as other schools (Mines did offer an in-state tuition discount), but waiving the application fee and essay certainly put them back into the conversation.

Finding 'Modern' Inspiration

Some of the sharpest insights regarding the college essay have come from ABC's Emmy-winning sitcom *Modern Family.*

In one episode, Haley Dunphy needs to write a college admissions essay, but she cannot think of any obstacles she has overcome. Naturally, she blames her mom Claire for her lack of material ("Gabby's mom's a hoarder—that essay practically writes itself!").

In order to help inspire her daughter, Claire takes Haley out to the woods, purportedly to show her an old tree, but once Haley gets out of the car, Claire drives off and leaves her eldest child to find her own way home. "There's your obstacle!" she screams as the family minivan takes off down the road in a cloud of dust.

A few years later, it was sister Alex's turn to come up with an essay for Harvard. Alex is the brilliant, talented, dutiful daughter, and she has a different problem than her older sister. Because she heard that Harvard likes a worldly perspective, Alex tries desperately to turn every moment of their family trip to Australia into an inspirational essay. Much to the annoyance of her family, she begins dictating potential essay ideas into her smartphone. A few gems: "Sometimes one must travel halfway across the globe to get the clearest view of home" and "What is a bridge? It's a connecter, a supporter, and sometimes, it's a metaphor...".

The Dunphy girls are no different than so many students who view the college essay as an *ordeal* instead of an *opportunity.* They resign themselves to thinking that either *they have nothing to write about* or they convince themselves that they *need to write about what they think the colleges want to hear.* Too many kids waste their opportunity on an essay that is either milquetoast or pretentious.

"DOC, I'M JUST HERE TO FIND A TOPIC FOR MY COLLEGE ESSAY"

Not-So-Easy Writer

There are a lot of books on the market about writing college essays, and if you really want to slog your way through hundreds of pages of dry prose that is chock full of sample essays most students would never write, then more power to you.

Some of these books offer "10 Easy Steps" to writing an essay. Please. These steps might sound simple, but there is nothing inherently easy about writing a college essay. It takes some work. And if you try using a template or formula to write your essay, then you are guaranteeing a copycat application as discussed in Chapter 4.

Reading a whole book about how to write an essay is no walk in the park. The college essay does not have a shortcut—if you want to attend a highly selective school, you must write one.

There are also dozens of books on the market featuring "Essays That Worked." These books claim to have actual college essays that got kids into college. A couple of young entrepreneurs even launched a website, AdmitSee, which pays college students about $200 to create a profile and post the essay that got them into their colleges.

Then AdmitSee charges high school students $49.99 a month for the Plus package (or $119.99 monthly for the Pro plan) so they can read the essays that allegedly worked.

GET REAL: Which is more likely: A student gets into college with a stellar application and an okay—or even subpar—essay, or a student gets into college with mediocre credentials and a brilliant essay? Just because someone got into Columbia, it does not mean the essay was the deciding factor. It might have been in spite of it. As some admissions officers explain: **A good essay can cure the sick, but it cannot raise the dead.**

If you want to read some essays that actually worked, go directly to the college websites. Many schools like Johns Hopkins share authentic essays (for free!) that were recommended by the admissions committee. Again, just because you read an essay you like does not mean you should imitate it.

The college essay is asking, *What are you all about?* Reply with a story.

Those Who Defend Everything, Defend Nothing

Essays are one of the main vehicles by which colleges learn about an applicant above and beyond the objective data and lists of extracurricular activities. It also feels the most like "the assignment" part of the application. Students have to write something new—it almost feels like a test.

Parents can get particularly neurotic when it comes to the essay, and their insecure, obedient students often listen to them, which results in a sterile version of what might have been.

I once had a student who was intellectually cool and interesting, but her essays were so wooden that they left splinters. I asked her why her essay was so dull, and she replied, "My parents won't leave my essay alone!" It turns out that mom and dad kept editing all the humanity out of her writing to the point that only bland prose remained.

I felt for this student, and her experience is fairly common. Some parents think the essay should run through a checklist of what-the-colleges-want-to-see, but the best essays tend to be the tip of the iceberg (as opposed to what Holden Caulfield would call "all that David Copperfield kind of crap" in *The Catcher in the Rye*). Students will sometimes complain that they cannot possibly tell their entire story in 650 words. I appreciate why students think that way, but that is not what the colleges are asking. Admissions officers think like Nirvana: "Here we are now, entertain us!"

On my desk sits a small tchotchke of Peter the Great. It is actually a bit of a prop for college counseling meetings. I will point to the miniature statue and say, "That is Peter the Great. He is here for two reasons. First, he is awesome. Second, he once said, 'He who defends everything, defends nothing.'" It is a perfect metaphor for the students who attempt to recount every curricular and extracurricular activity since middle school on their essay. You simply cannot cover it all.

Shopping for Essays at Costco

Technology makes it easy for college essays to go viral.

In 1990, high school student Hugh Gallagher had his moment of fame after he wrote a satirical college essay that was eventually published by Harper's. In the essay, the "applicant" makes a series of hilariously outrageous claims that today sound a lot like the Dos Equis Most Interesting Man in the World ("I woo women with my sensuous and godlike trombone playing"). The essay is a bit of an urban legend. Gallagher didn't actually use this hilarious prose as his own college essay (it was written for a creative writing contest), but he did submit it to NYU as a sample of his writing skills, and he did get accepted.

In 2016, high school senior Brittany Stinson reportedly got into a whole bunch of Ultras in part because of her essay about exploring Costco as a child. But if you read the internet (*Business Insider* used the clickbait headline "This essay got a high-school senior into 5 Ivy League schools and Stanford"), it sounded as though the essay was the *only* reason that Brittany was accepted by these schools (she eventually chose Stanford). It's a fine essay. Read it if you like. Not every student can pull off an essay like that. Still, as good as it is, it wasn't the reason she got in: Brittany was valedictorian (with a 4.0 GPA), she is fluent in Portuguese (in part thanks to her Brazilian-born mother), she took eight AP courses, *and* she attended summer programs to study astrophysics. Yeah, Brittany was getting into those schools with or without the Costco essay.

GET REAL: Yes, the essay is important, but it's not as mystical as many students and parents perceive. Academics come first in admissions.

Too Many Cooks

On the other end of the spectrum is the kid who absolutely will not let his parents (or anyone!) read any essays before submitting them. This student is like the attorney who defends himself in court—he has a fool for a client.

Ultimately the student is the one going to college, but parents need to be part of the application process. Finding the right balance makes all the difference.

Parents: Do not hover. Stay involved, but do not micromanage. Believe it or not, colleges can tell when adults have (co)-written an essay (usually it involves multiple semicolons and other tell-tale grammatical and syntactical flourishes like putting two spaces after a period).

When your essay is written by a half-dozen people, like a Transformers movie, it might have all kinds of explosions and excitement, but it will not win any awards and it might cause a few headaches.

From the outset, everyone needs to agree that essays will be shared—if not with a parent, then at least with a trusted college counselor, teacher, or tutor—but you should probably keep the rest of the adults (and most of your friends) out of the loop.

GET REAL: The essay is subjective. Different people might love the same essay for vastly different reasons. Ask a college counselor and an English teacher to look it over and you should be good to go. Your "mom's friend who is good at writing" is a highly dubious source of expertise on college essays.

Winter is Coming

Students should write their essays somewhere between the last day of their junior year (too soon?) and December 31 (for masochists only), yet there will be a lot going on in those seven months that will determine when you should write your essay.

One school of thought says to wait until the end of summer to write about something fresh and amazing that happened during break. And if you've got an interesting job, internship, or trip planned, a magical essay may indeed materialize. But Labor Day will arrive sooner than you think, fall is chock full of classes and activities, and Winter is Coming....

Instead, start the writing *process* in June. Trust me, students need to get their primary essay done over the summer before they start their senior year. This primary essay might end up functioning as several essays, including one for the Coalition Application, the Common App and in-state essays like those found on ApplyTexas. If you can reuse an essay, all the better.

Convincing students to begin writing college essays right after they complete their grueling junior year is a tough sell. One of my students even said to her parents, "The more you harp on me about the college applications, the farther away I'm going to apply."

Filling out all those college applications is a part-time job. If you do it right, it might not only get you accepted, but it could also earn you some scholarship money, and then you will not need an actual part-time job.

Even if you are going to Malaysia to set up an orphanage/hospital/performing arts center and will be gone all summer, try to build in some time to at least write the

Common App essay and one or two of the shorter supplemental essays for your state school or definite first-choice college.

PRO TIP: If you start writing over the summer, be sure that the essay topics have been posted for the next school year. The Common App usually updates its prompts in the spring, but individual colleges might not let you know their new prompts until July or August. My younger son was not happy with me when we discovered that many of the Wake Forest supplemental essays had been changed in July after he had already written the answers to the old prompts.

Hot Topic

Before you start making a list of potential topics from which to choose writing an essay, it's wise to actually read over the entire Common App and any other applications you plan on completing.

You want to give colleges an idea of what's important in your life. Grades, athletics, and certain activities are easy to highlight on the application, but depending on your extracurricular activities and outside interests, the application itself might not give you the adequate opportunity to show what's most important to you.

If you are involved in something that isn't likely to get noticed on the application, then how can colleges know it's a vital aspect of your being unless you tell them?

PRO TIP: Many families assume the essay has to be something unusually remarkable or life-changing, yet some of the best essays are written on seemingly pedestrian topics.

My older son became an Eagle Scout after his freshman year, which is impressive enough, but I have taught a lot of Eagle Scouts, and Scouting isn't necessarily an important part of who they are. Sure, it is a long-term commitment, but for many Scouts, their parents had a lot to do with them sticking with the program and earning the recognition. And even then, many Scouts just barely manage to get the paperwork in at the last minute before their 18th birthday.

What impressed me about Zach's involvement with Scouting is that I never once went on a campout with him and rarely attended meetings. It's what he wanted to do. And long after he obtained Scouting's highest honor, he stayed actively involved, becoming an Assistant Patrol Leader and then Senior Patrol Leader *after* becoming an Eagle. He even earned a Bronze Palm, a Gold Palm, and the National Outdoor Award for completing 125 days of camping. There simply was no place on the Common App to express how important the Boy Scout experience was, so his decision to write about Scouting for his Common App essay was not just obvious, it was necessary.

Colleges often ask for an essay that explores your *background, identity, interest* or *talent*, and if your identity is inexorably linked to your interests and talents but would otherwise be underrepresented on the application, then make sure you write about it in some way, somehow, in the essay.

If your accomplishments and interests are already adequately delineated on the application, then you are blissfully free to write about any topic of your choosing.

But where to find inspiration? Meat Loaf once sang, "I know you're looking for a ruby in a mountain of rocks, but there ain't no Coupe de Ville hiding at the bottom of a Cracker Jack box."

Students often know what they want to write about. And they know how they want to write it. And they want it to be done quickly and painlessly.

Two out of three ain't bad.

Eureka!

Once upon a time, on an ordinary day in April, a junior girl came into my classroom to talk about a paper she was writing for my class, but before we began discussing countercultural literature, I asked her how track season was going.

She said that she liked running cross country better than track. When I asked her why, she explained, "In track, you just run around in circles and are always under pressure, always looking over your shoulder to see where your competition is. In cross country, you're part of a team, not just an individual runner, and you get to see changing scenery."

I looked at her and said, "Do you realize what you've just done? You've come up with your college essay."

Students have these kinds of revelations every day—they just don't realize that they can be used to let the world know exactly who they are.

This girl was a good student who excelled in dance and long-distance running. I knew she would be looking at small liberal arts colleges, not big state schools. Her preference of cross country over track was representative of her desire to attend a school where she could become part of a close-knit community (with a bucolic setting). She was not looking for a giant, bustling school or one in a large urban center.

She wound up attending Smith, which was a perfect fit.

Sporty Essays

Another student, this time a boy who played multiple sports, conferenced with me about his college essay. It was a typically middling story about doing good deeds as a volunteer in Costa Rica, but it lacked anything about who he was or why he felt compelled to serve others. His essay was perfunctory, yet devoid of feeling and meaning, just like the majority of first draft essays I read.

I knew the Costa Rica essay had to be scrapped, but I also knew that he couldn't just write an essay about his participation in sports either. The "Sports as a Metaphor for Life" essay can work wonders by getting sporty kids (but by no means future NCAA athletes) to find attributes in athletics and make connections to other aspects of their lives.

This boy was the punter for the football team and the goalie for the soccer team— not the usual combo. I asked him what those two positions had in common, and after we talked for a while, the light clicked ON.

He realized that punters and goalies are literally and figuratively "the last line of defense." They will never score by design, and they shoulder a disproportionate amount of blame for having a punt blocked or surrendering a goal, even if it was caused by a missed blocking assignment or a breakdown on defense.

The goalie-punter realized that he is the kind of person who is drawn to activities that offer little glory and much responsibility, whether it's sports or community service. He is the glue who holds it together, not the quarterback or striker who gets to pump his fists in triumph. He is the one trying to make sure things do not get out of control.

This was another great kid—funny, responsible, and friendly—and he attended the University of Maryland.

The App is Common, Your Essay Should Not Be

From its inception, the Common App offered five essay choices, but in 2017 they added two additional prompts and modified some of the old prompts. Do not be surprised if they continue to evolve every year. The latest incarnations are revealed in the spring, so there should be plenty of time for students to prepare.

The 2019-2020 essay prompts are:

1. Some students have a background, identity, interest, or talent that is so meaningful they believe their application would be incomplete without it. If this sounds like you, then please share your story.

2. The lessons we take from obstacles we encounter can be fundamental to later success. Recount a time when you faced a challenge, setback or failure. How did it affect you, and what did you learn from the experience?

3. Reflect on a time when you questioned or challenged a belief or idea. What prompted your thinking? What was the outcome?

4. Describe a problem you've solved or a problem you'd like to solve. It can be an intellectual challenge, a research query, an ethical dilemma—anything that is of personal importance, no matter the scale. Explain its significance to you and what steps you took or could be taken to identify a solution.

5. Discuss an accomplishment, event or realization that sparked a period of personal growth and a new understanding or yourself of others.

6. Describe a topic, idea or concept you find so engaging that it makes you lose all track of time. Why does it captivate you? What or who do you turn to when you want to learn more? [New in 2017]

7. Share an essay on any topic of your choice. It can be one you've already written, one that responds to a different prompt, or one of your own design. [New in 2017]

According to the Common App website, in January 2016 (before they added the two extra prompts) there were over 800,000 unique applicants. Almost half (47 percent) chose to write about their "background, identity, interest or talent" (Essay 1); 22 percent wrote about an "accomplishment or event" (Essay 5); 17 percent detailed a lesson from failure (Essay 2); a paltry 10 percent wrote about a problem solved (Essay 4), and a measly 4 percent wrote about an idea or belief challenged (Essay 3).

During the 2018-2019 application year, those results had changed. The free choice option jumped to the top with 24.1 percent, followed by Essay 5 (23.7 percent) and Essay 2 (21.1 percent).

Let's take a closer look at your options before trying to outthink the competition.

Prompt 1 essentially asks students to write about what the college needs to know that they cannot figure out by reading your application and looking at your transcript. This prompt is best for someone with a specific, dynamic story, especially if that story details any kind of racial, gender identity, socio-economic, blended, or non-traditional backgrounds. A few years ago, writing about being a **third culture kid** (someone raised outside of their parents' culture for many years) was unique. Today you may need more.

There is a good reason why this essay is still popular—you can do just about anything with it. Do not ignore this essay because of its popularity, but do not to waste the opportunity by writing something boring or predictable.

Prompt 2 was modified in 2017 (using the word *obstacle* instead of *failure*. And thank goodness! Students did not know quite how to handle talking about failure, so they often wrote essays about the failure of others to recognize how special they are. Too often students used this essay to explain the injustice of not being chosen as captain of the lacrosse team, editor of the newspaper, or winner of a Scholastic Art Award. Don't be that kid.

Whether you are writing about a challenge, setback, or failure, do not make excuses, do not sound bitter, and do not blame anyone else for your shortcomings. Whatever tactic you choose, please do not write about losing a sporting event only to practice harder, come together as a team, and eventually win The Big Game. If you are a recruited scholarship athlete, fine, write about sports. Otherwise, you are missing an opportunity.

Equally ineffective is a trite story that can be summarized thusly: *I came. I failed. I learned so much about myself.*

Use this prompt if you want to talk about something with intrinsic value (not extrinsic value like getting an award or earning a title or winning an election). Talk about your quest to build the perfect battle bot, cosplay outfit, or tree house. Make it about you. And if you must write about sports, talk about the satisfaction that comes from competition, not winning.

PRO TIP: Prompt 2 is so cool—and scares so many students. **Colleges do not want certainty; they want curiosity.** Regardless of the activity, you know you did it right when you succeeded, but what did you learn when you didn't?

Prompt 3 has been broadened to include not only when a student challenged a belief or idea, but also when they questioned previously held views. The old prompt seemed to require a story about students confronting others, which is something students are often unwilling or unable to do. Thankfully, the current prompt is more cerebral, allowing for a difference of opinion without all that messy conflict.

The prompt is still tricky because it has the potential to get into topics that are generally not discussed in polite company—religion and politics. Remember, the Common App is for *all* the schools you are applying to, so you cannot tailor one for Villanova and another for Reed College.

There will certainly be the temptation to discuss the 2016 presidential election or the presidency of Donald Trump, but if you want to write about politics, you should know that while college employees tend to skew liberal, you cannot be certain that your reader will be in agreement with your politics. As long as you are thoughtful and not incendiary, you can talk about the government, but proceed with caution.

Need some additional inspiration? Since the days of Edward R. Murrow in the 1950s, National Public Radio has featured "This I Believe" essays (you can find many at thisibelieve.org) and read some for yourself. When done right, they are an awesome way to let a college see who you are. When done wrong, applicants come across as close-minded and dogmatic.

Prompt 4 replaced an essay about an applicant's "Special Place" from 2014 (and remains unchanged in 2019). Most people were happy about that change. The current essay should be workable for just about any student. Everyone encounters problems, and the way a person goes about solving the problem (and what they consider a problem in the first place) says a lot more about that person than whether or not the solution was effective.

Do not write about the struggle of driving a used minivan while your friends all have the new Lexus. Avoid essays about the struggle to find something to write about for your college essay. Basically, stay away from anything that makes you sound like Rory Gilmore.

It is a bit surprising that only ten percent of applicants chose this prompt a few years ago since it allows students to show vulnerability, but with a happy ending. Essay Topic 4 was partially created with STEM students in mind. If you are one of these students, what do you want to solve using STEM disciplines?

Prompt 5 was overhauled for 2017. For years this prompt focused on an event, formal or informal, that marked a perceived transition to adulthood. Students often wrote about formal rites of passage like a Bar Mitzvah, Quinceañera, Confirmation, or Eagle Scout ceremony, or they struggled to find an informal moment like taking more responsibility within their household, getting a driver license or voting for the first time.

The revised prompt is so broad that you could write about practically anything that explores a moment in which you had an epiphany about yourself, which helps explain its popularity.

Prompt 6 was new for 2017, and it's a winner. The prompt wants to know what gets you excited (educationally, of course). This should not be a "passion paper." You might be passionate about theater, water polo, or organic chemistry, but the prompt wants you to discuss an activity that makes time feel insignificant. Basically, what do you do that you love so much that you do it freely, without the expectation of reward or recompense?

An admissions officer from Tufts once described a successful essay as follows: If your best friend read 100 anonymous essays and could pick yours out of the stack, then you know it works.

Warning: Old-school admissions officers will not appreciate essays about playing video games. Ditto for binge-watching Netflix.

Writing on topics such as reading, writing, running, or working out are perfectly fine, but an essay about how reading a good book makes you lose track of time is not going to stand out.

Whatever you choose, avoid writing about how Activity X led to the discovery of one of the Four Noble Truths (*Golf taught me patience*).

Prompt 7 marked the return of the "write your own" essay prompt.

It's unlikely that the free-choice essay would not fit into one of the first six topics, but if you have a really specific subject that you would like to discuss or a (somewhat) off-the-wall prompt to explore like the ones found on the University of Chicago application, then this catch-all topic is for you.

PRO TIP: If you are interested in writing an essay, people will be interested in reading it. If you are resentful, exasperated, unprepared, or unenthusiastic, your reader might feel the same.

Do not be fooled by the name. The Common App should make you seem extraordinary, but not narcissistic.

Ann Lee, co-founder of a college prep business, offered this advice specifically for Asian-American students who want to set themselves apart: "Everyone is in orchestra and plays piano. Everyone plays tennis. Everyone wants to be a doctor and write about immigrating to America. You can't get in with these cliché applications."

Although Lee was speaking about the Asian-American experience, anyone can appreciate that there are thousands of applicants with similar qualifications and qualities, and the essay is the golden ticket to stand out.

Supplemental Essays

Many of the Ultras want more than just the Common App essay. Some request another long essay, others require several shorter (250-350 words) responses.

The University of Chicago requires one primary essay, one optional essay (translation: it's required) and one supplemental essay inspired by current UChicago students.

For the 2016-2017 application, supplemental essays included this gem: *Joan of Arkansas. Queen Elizabeth Cady Stanton. Babe Ruth Bader Ginsburg. Mash up a historical figure with a new time period, environment, location, or occupation, and tell us their story.*

The irony is that while UChicago is often derisively referred to as "The Place Where Fun Goes to Die," their writing prompts are entertaining and inventive—which scares the bejeezus out of potential applicants because there is no "right" way to tackle them.

Rice University has always included a blank box on their application and requested that applicants fill in the box with "an image of something that appeals to you." This nebulous, open-ended prompt baffles many applicants, and those that include pictures of actual rice or Uncle Ben (or attach pieces of uncooked rice!) are not helping themselves. One of the coolest answers I have ever seen to the Rice box prompt was from a student who found an intersection in Houston with Rice Boulevard and a street with her first name and sent a picture of herself standing underneath the signs.

As we have seen, the more writing that is required on the application, the fewer students will apply. If you notice a change in the number (or length) of questions from the previous year's application, that's an indicator of whether or not the college is looking for more (or fewer) applicants.

The 'Why Us' Essay

If you are applying to a selective college, you are probably going to see a variation of this prompt: Why _____?

Colleges want to see just how much homework you've done in choosing where to apply. If all you know about the school can be found on their website or brochure: (*We have three acapella groups, offer a variety of study abroad options, and have a great library!*), then you will not be able to fake an essay about why you want to apply. Vagueness will sink you.

Do not recycle the Why Us essay for multiple colleges. Many schools have similar features (I counted three campus tour guides who mentioned a tradition about how kissing a person at a specific location on campus will result in marriage), but there is a significant difference between Dartmouth and Brown, so do not write a generic essay in which you talk in glittering generalities about how "your college has everything I need to reach my full potential." And nothing will get you denied quicker than double-dipping on your essays and forgetting to change that reference to MIT in the third paragraph when you are writing to Caltech.

The Why Us essay allows you to mention if you have any family or friends at the school, if you have visited campus and taken a tour, and what exactly they can offer you to meet your goals.

PRO TIP: This essay is vital at any college asking for it. Do not talk about rankings, reputation, or prestige. Do not write something that is so bland that it could be almost any college (e.g., "When I learned you had undergraduate research opportunities, it piqued my interest!") Name drop like crazy: buildings, clubs, classes, professors, programs, etc. **Show 'em that you know 'em.**

Keep in mind that members of the admissions committee work on campus, so there is no reason to tell them what they already know, like describing how gorgeous the campus is or citing the faculty-to-student ratio (just don't!). If the information is already on their website or in a brochure, do not mention it in your essay, but you absolutely should discuss specific aspects of the college that you find appealing.

Just like the Common App essay, the purpose of the Why Us essay is to talk about you. So while you will certainly mention the college and its location in the Why Us essay, be sure to describe just how well you will fit in at that specific school.

Here is an actual answer to the supplemental essay question "Why do you wish to come to Harvard":

> The reasons that I have for wishing to go to Harvard are several. I feel that Harvard can give me a better background and a better liberal education than any other university. I have always wanted to go there, as I have felt that it is not just another college, but is a university with something definite to offer. Then too, I would like to go to the same college as my father. To be a "Harvard man" is an enviable distinction, and one that I sincerely hope I shall attain.

That vague essay was recycled almost verbatim for the applicant's Princeton application as well. Today an essay like this would not work, but 17-year-old John Fitzgerald Kennedy did not need to expend too much thought crafting a brilliant answer to this prompt back in 1935. Kennedy had some pretty strong credentials and connections going for him, but you will need to do a bit more.

Even if you are not required to write a Why Us essay, you should still come up with an answer for each school since you are likely to be asked that very question during your interview (see Chapter 10).

If you have not figured it out by now, the Why Us essay is a way for colleges to see if you are really interested in them and have done your research (or are you just name brand shopping because the college was on some "Best Of" list?).

GET REAL: Think about it like this: You are an admissions officer at a highly selective school that requires applicants to write a Why Us essay. Your dean asks you to keep in mind the following: Does this person want to study here because of what we offer, or do they want to study here because we are a "name" school?

If you seriously cannot answer the Why Us essay, perhaps you should take that college off your list and focus on the schools that really interest you.

The Unbearable Rightness of Writing

Regardless of what kind of essay you have to write, there are ways to improve your chances to impress the admissions officers.

For every essay, there are two narrators: (1) you writing the essay during the writing process and (2) you when the story happened. Even if you are writing about something that happened last month, you are a different person writing the essay than you were when you ran your first marathon, drove your younger siblings to school for the first time, or voted in your first presidential election. You have perspective. You have changed. Let your reader see how much you know about yourself by showing the difference between who you are now and who you were then.

Like the ghosts in Charles Dickens's *A Christmas Carol*, you should not only mention Past You and Present You, but try to give colleges a glimpse at Future You. After all, when you apply to college, you are not only looking back at your high school accomplishments, but you are also projecting forward to see what the college experience will do for you over the next four years—or even a lifetime.

Three Big Essay Topics

The Big Three life-changing events for most students are Death, Moving, and Divorce, and while these are not specifically addressed in the Common App prompts, students may find themselves wanting to write on these topics or use them for scholarship or supplemental essays. Mom and Dad are often proponents of writing about The Big Thing. A few words of caution before using any of these topics:

Death: In high school, the most common brushes with death are grandparents and pets. It's a tricky topic because these essays can be super depressing to read and emotionally difficult for the student to write. Teenagers have difficulty putting death into perspective for a college essay (News flash: It's also difficult for adults). That being said, the death of a parent, sibling, mentor, friend, or public figure may very well be a defining moment in a young person's life. If you have come to grips with the ordeal, then writing about death can work. If the trauma is still fresh or the student is still working through grief, then it is probably better to write about something else.

The biggest problem with writing about the deceased is that too often the student spends so much time writing about how special that person was that they neglect to mention themselves. In the end, admissions officers learn more about Grandpa, not the student.

For aspiring doctors, there is a tendency to write about the loss of a loved one and how it inspired them to work towards a future in medicine. Origin stories about how you became a costumed crime fighter following the death of beloved family member are fine if you're Bruce Wayne or Peter Parker, otherwise you should avoid this overused trope.

Moving: Leaving your old, safe environment and moving to a strange new world (especially if it's another country) is a worthy topic, but be warned that it is pretty common. Do you have anything new to say about what it's like to be the new kid in town? Got anything besides a tepid story about losing your sense of direction? These essays should avoid formulaic devices.

If your name is Cady Heron and you just moved to the suburbs of Illinois after living in Africa for 12 years, then you have a fantastic essay topic (and the backstory of *Mean Girls*), otherwise fish-out-of-water stories are fairly pedestrian.

And guess what? You are going to be moving to college in a few months—if you sound like you had such a difficult time adjusting to a new environment in high school, then colleges may think they are doing you a favor by nixing you since you will be spared the trauma of moving all over again.

Divorce: This is another potentially painful experience, and one topic that is tough to write about, especially if one (or both) parents will be reading it. Some students might think that being a child of divorce will help their chances by eliciting sympathy, but it really will not set you apart, and it's not the kind of topic most students are comfortable sharing.

SEMI-PRO TIP: I never thought I would have to tell students this, but I have seen so many essays in which people write about their boyfriends or girlfriends that I have to caution against it. While it may be true that Brett or Ashlee is the most important person in your life, look for a topic with a bit more gravitas.

Accidents Will Happen

Accidents and injuries are another mainstay of the college essay because it fits the bill for the "overcoming obstacles" essay. Whether it's rehabbing from a torn ACL that occurred while playing lacrosse or breaking your coccyx after falling off a hoverboard, these essays certainly examine one's resilience. As with all college essays, the key is not to get too bogged down in the minutia of the incident (or the recovery) but to gain perspective from the ordeal.

For some, accidents and injuries are temporary obstacles, but for many students, medical issues are an ongoing ordeal. Try to elicit understanding about the situation without crossing into maudlin territory.

My Grandparents Were Amazing, Too!

Many, many (!) students default to writing about their grandparents when colleges ask students to "describe someone who has had an influence on you and describe that influence." First, it is totally acceptable to write about your grandparents, and lord knows there are countless folks who have raised their grandchildren because of family hardship and circumstance. These people should be celebrated, but maybe not in a college essay.

Students routinely pick their grandma or grandpa for this topic, and it is certainly not forbidden, but most admissions officers have been there, done that. I have read plenty of grandparent essays that are fantastic, but unfortunately some of them make the mistake of *only* discussing the grandparent and *not* their influence on the student.

So, you can write about your grandparents, but understand that these essays are fairly routine. And if you do write about meemaw or paw-paw, remember to *bring it back to you.* The prompt is really, "How did this person influence you?" It is not: "Tell me how awesome someone in your life is."

On a Mission from God: Rethinking the Mission Trip Essay

To paraphrase Spinal Tap, there is a fine line between empathetic and condescending. Over the past 20 years, community service has evolved from an act of selflessness to an obligatory résumé-filler. There is no amount of volunteerism and community service that will allow you to stand out from the crowd, yet you may fear that having none makes you look like some kind of heartless slacker.

If you survey most high school students, volunteerism is something that they know they should engage in, but it's an activity that they don't actually want to do unless persuaded by someone else—kind of like writing thank-you notes.

PRO TIP: Write thank-you notes to everyone you encounter in the college process. The local college rep that came to your school at lunch or on College Night—write them a letter. The teachers who write your rec letters are most deserving of a note (and a Starbucks gift card never hurt either). And definitely send short, polite hand-written letters to the regional college rep since that's who will be fighting for you in committee. Prove that you have manners and are willing to go the extra mile for them because you just might need them to go to bat for you. And yes, everything you send to the college, including thank-you notes, are put in your file. Good manners never hurt.

So are volunteer hours created equal? Is working in your local food bank or church the same as traveling to Micronesia to help the sick or build elementary schools?

There is a growing school of thought that says charity begins at home, so all those trips to India, Africa and Central America (mockingly dubbed **voluntourism** by detractors) smack of privilege and can be perceived as expensive, pre-packaged essay starters.

Let's assume you have the purest of intentions when you volunteer to help build houses in Guatemala. You even raise money to fund the trip yourself and you are not piggybacking the journey with a Royal Caribbean cruise or side excursion to the

Bahamas. How do you ensure that you do not come across as a spoiled, sheltered American?

GET REAL: Community service, much like other extracurricular activities, is not required for admission. It will not be "the thing" that gets you in, but it is an excellent source of good karma.

I have read so many essays from well-meaning kids who went on a school or church mission trip, and their big lesson is often as follows: *I used to take my sheltered life for granted, but after seeing how the noble people of _____ lived, I have come to appreciate everything I have.*

On the surface, this may sound okay, perhaps even noble, but it reeks of American exceptionalism and is fairly condescending to the people that these students were ostensibly there to help.

Another problematic essays starter: *How we introduced the people to [insert name of deity or religion here] and showed them the Path of Love.*

Unless you are applying exclusively to parochial schools that might appreciate the work you are doing in the Name of the Lord, writing about converting the natives is a dicey proposition. Colleges are, by their very nature, fairly liberal environments, so if you position yourself as a zealot (even one who does remarkably good deeds), you might give the college ample reason to believe you might be more comfortable at a more conservative (i.e., religious) institution.

And then there are essays about volunteering that focus on all the hardships students encounter like no running water, no air conditioning, and no Wi-Fi. If the trip lasts just a week or two and the takeaway is that you missed your smartphone and these poor people do not get to shower regularly, then you might come across as sheltered and self-centered.

It is absolutely possible to do nice things for others, just try not to sound tone deaf in the process.

PRO TIP: Community service in your home town could be perceived as more compelling than going overseas since the admissions officer might wonder why you chose to go so far away to volunteer. Helping abroad is not "better" than helping locally. This is by no means a strict rule—a student might have a passion for an international cause, which is fine, but do not assume that volunteering internationally improves your chances.

Going out on a Limb: The Reach Essay

Students should always apply to a range of schools: a few reach schools, several target schools and a few safety schools. In the old days, you could tailor an essay for each individual school, but the Common App includes the same essay for every school.

If you have all the credentials for the most selective schools (or are somehow overqualified), then do not write an edgy essay. Play it safe and get the job done.

Students applying to reach schools might consider something more aggressive in order to get the attention of the committee, and there are plenty of supplemental essay prompts that will allow you to accomplish this. Please note that there is a fine line between edgy and inappropriate. In Frank Bruni's *Where You Go Is Not Who You'll Be*, he mentions an essay written by a young lady who admitted to peeing on herself rather than excusing herself during a particularly enthralling discussion with a teacher.

You may have been taught that Honesty Is the Best Policy, but when it comes to college applications, Discretion Is the Better Part of Valor.

I have read college essays that mention drug use, drunk driving, sexual promiscuity, and self-mutilation. Even if the underlying message is ultimately positive, oversharing or pushing the envelope sends up a warning for admissions officers that the student might have an underdeveloped social filter.

PRO TIP: Watch out for oversharing. If you would not share your story with your entire school at an assembly, then you should probably keep it private. It is also astonishing how many students write about losing their virginity. Please don't go there.

There may be some admissions officers who appreciate your bravery and candor in broaching a serious topic. Certainly it depends. It's not necessarily the subject matter that's a concern but rather the way you handle dealing with sensitive issues. Ultimately, the college essay is not an appropriate place to work out deep-seated psychological issues—be careful not to give too much sensitive information.

The Embellished Essay

Naturally, you want to put yourself in the best light possible when applying to college, but there is a line that should never be crossed. **Do not lie about your accomplishments.**

Repeat: **Do Not Lie on Your Application.**

Do not say you are the vice president of a club when you really just went to one meeting (*How would they ever know?*). Do not claim you spent 20 hours a week doing volunteer work when you did 20 for the entire semester. Colleges *do* check the math, and sometimes, after crunching the numbers, the colleges determine that miraculously some applicants manage to cram 30 hours of school and activities into 24 hours.

GET REAL: Admissions officers are allotted 24 hours a day, and they have to sleep at some point. If you appear to have more than 24 hours a day accounted for in your application, then they will be confused, skeptical, and jealous.

Colleges receive thousands of applications, and their B.S. detector is finely tuned. Schools have an array of resources to fact-check your story (they might be older than you, but they do know how to use the internet). And a growing number of colleges automatically flag a small percentage of applications to check for veracity.

Even if you do manage to get away with some seemingly harmless exaggerations, it's often just a matter of time before the lie is discovered.

Busted!

In 2007, Adam Wheeler was accepted as a transfer student at Harvard by plagiarizing his essays as well as faking a transcript and SAT scores, and he might have gotten away with it, except Wheeler also used the same falsified information to apply for a Rhodes and Fulbright Scholarship. In 2011, he was sentenced to two-and-a-half years in prison and 10 years' probation on fraud charges.

In 2010, the Penn State business program began using Turnitin, a company that checks for plagiarism, which became necessary after they discovered that 30 applicants had lifted passages from the same online article on "principled leadership." *Isn't it ironic, don't you think?* Today hundreds of schools use Turnitin to catch plagiarists.

Lest you think that lying about one's qualifications is limited to students, there is the case of Marilee Jones, the MIT director of admissions, who resigned in 2007 when she admitted that she lied about having an undergraduate and master's degree. She had neither.

And for you sports fans, Notre Dame hired away Georgia Tech football coach George O'Leary in 2001, and he resigned just five days later when it came to light that he lied about being a three-year letterman at the University of New Hampshire (he never even played one game and only attended school there for two years). O'Leary also claimed that he had a master's degree from NYU (he only took two classes).

Passion Play: Turn Your Interests into a Compelling Narrative

James Dean became a movie legend portraying a Rebel Without a Cause (still an amazing movie—go watch it), but if you are writing a college essay, you need to get a cause. A real one.

College admissions officers are often called gatekeepers. Your job as the applicant is to open the gate—and the essay is your key. When writing the essay, be specific about what you like and what you are like. Do not assume that the admissions committee knows everything about you. What you might think of as boring might be fascinating to Admissions.

Here are just a few topics that might seem humdrum to you, but might be novel, even intriguing to colleges:

- Perhaps you belong to the Future Farmers of America. You raise pigs that you feed and groom daily before taking them to the Livestock Show every year.
- Maybe you are the one-in-2,000 who associates colors with letter and numbers, or possibly music. You might not even know that you have *synesthesia*, but it could make for a fascinating essay.
- Or maybe you place your Starbucks order under a different alias every time. Why? What's your story?

What you do is less important than why you do it. Make your interest infectious. Let the reader see why you are so enthralled with whatever it is you do.

PRO TIP: Talk about your passion all you like, but do not use the phrase "find my passion" because no one actually talks like that. In fact, leave the word "passion" out of all your essays completely. Do not *say* you are passionate—prove it!

Lighten Up

Do you consider yourself a member of the "Geek" Orthodox Church due to your deep and abiding love of all things related to Star Trek? Do you have a weekend job entertaining at children's birthday parties dressed as Elsa from *Frozen*? Do you design your own clothes inspired by *Sailor Moon* and travel the Comic-Con circuit showing off your work? Whatever you are enthusiastic about, topics like these will make for a better reading experience than vague essays about seemingly weightier topics.

Final Thought: When an admissions officer has to "present," the admissions committee has already gone over your transcript, so they delve into the essay. Occasionally, the essay is the determining factor. When the committee asks the admissions officer to read the essay aloud, you want your voice in the room. And when an admissions officer gets to present, look out. It's game on.

THE NUTS AND BOLTS OF ESSAY WRITING

CHAPTER 8

I think of all the education that I missed,
But then my homework was never quite like this.

— *Van Halen, "Hot for Teacher"*

THE KEY TO ALL COLLEGE ESSAYS is best expressed by the ancient Greek aphorism "Know Thyself."

If you know who you are and why you do what you do, then you can write on just about any topic. Colleges cannot get to know you if you do not know yourself.

The High School Hero's Journey

Every high school student learns the Hero's Journey at some point in their English classes. And whether we are talking about Odysseus or Sir Gawain, Harry Potter or Katniss Everdeen, the hero has a somewhat predictable pattern of inaction, doubt, decision, and action.

You will encounter the same cycle in writing the college essay. In case you have not studied Joseph Campbell's seminal hero theory, here is the condensed version and how you, as the hero of your own narrative, might tackle the college application process:

1. Ordinary World: *You are a high school student just after your third year.*

2. Call to Adventure: *You decide to apply to college!*

3. Refusal of the Call: *I don't want to do the application now, mom!*

4. Meeting the Mentor: *Ms. Counsell, where do you think I should apply?*

5. Crossing the Threshold: *Here is the intro for my essay "Overcoming Ringworm."*

6. Tests, Allies & Enemies: *The admissions tests, the teachers and counselors writing your rec letters, and everyone else applying to the same schools as you.*

7. Approach: *Deadlines.*

8. Ordeal, Death and Rebirth: *Finishing the application process. Taking more tests. Keeping up your grades. Burnout. Getting up and going back to school every day, just like Sisyphus rolling his boulder up the hill.*

9. Reward: *Congratulations, your essay is done and you don't need to take the ACT again!*

10. The Road Back: *Discovering all those things you used to enjoy when you weren't so busy with applications.*

11. Resurrection: *(Often occurs after applications are completed over winter break) I'm back!*

12. Return with Elixir: *Congratulations, you have been accepted! (Elixir optional)*

In the Coen Brothers brilliant film *O Brother, Where Art Thou?*, itself an adaptation of Homer's *Odyssey*, the Blind Seer delivers a prophecy to a trio of adventurers at the outset of their journey: "I cannot tell you how long this road shall be, but fear not the obstacles in your path, for fate has vouchsafed your reward." Those who embrace the Hero's Journey and accept the Call to Adventure will find that fate (if not the odds) will favor them as well.

Quality Control

I know what some of you are thinking—you've made B's in English and got a 650 on SAT Critical Reading section, but if you write a killer essay, then you can make up for your somewhat spotty performance.

There's just one problem: Pristine, publication-worthy essays are typically not written by B-students with good, but not great, standardized test scores.

If you do manage to craft a perfect essay, an admissions officer might doubt the authenticity of your writing and assume that you may have received help from a thesaurus, your parents, or a paid consultant. Possibly all three.

What's worse, your reader might assume your essay has been plagiarized.

The quality of your essay should match the quality of the entire application. If your essay is far better than your supplements and short-answer replies—as your grades, ACT score, and rec letters would suggest—then colleges will suspect that you didn't create the essay on your own. And if, for the sake of argument, they do believe all your essays are genuine, then they would be justified in wondering why you have failed to live up to the potential of a person who can write such fantastic essays. Either way, it is problematic.

Some independent educational consultants know about this conundrum and are so good at disguising the fact that the student received outside assistance on an essay that they intentionally include small grammatical and formatting errors to throw suspicious admissions officers off the scent.

It all comes down to one simple rule: **Do not try to write better than you can write.**

You cannot write better than you can write any more than you can be taller than you are high. Sure, you can create the illusion of height by wearing high heels or platform shoes, but the more lift they give you, the more obvious (and unstable) the deception becomes. If you went to basketball tryouts wearing stilts, it would become laughably apparent that you are not really 8-foot-6.

The corollary to this rule: **Write as well as you can.**

If you are a B-student, you cannot turn in the perfect essay—unless it becomes apparent why you are a great writer. If you have won numerous creative writing contests, and you have been published in a literary magazine, and your English teacher rec letter references your brilliant prose, then you are probably covered.

Of course, there may be mitigating circumstances. Maybe you have dyslexia and/or dysgraphia, which make it tougher for you on vocabulary quizzes or affect your handwriting so it is difficult for teachers to read. At least you would have an explanation for being a talented writer and not making an A (colleges do recognize that there is more to being a good writer than getting an A in English). You just might be a brilliant writer who refuses to do any reading (but do not mention that either).

Just Like the Little Mermaid, You Need to Find Your Voice

Talk to any high school student (as long as it's not about college). Go ahead, they don't bite.

Students have a way of talking that is often quite engaging. They can carry on a conversation that is deep, intriguing, and sometimes downright scintillating. Now try getting that same student to write you an essay on the very topic you just discussed with them. It will not read the same.

It's often stiff. Stilted. Riddled with clichés and stuffed with useless details. And it sounds nothing like their real voice. When educators talk about finding one's voice, they mean that one's written work sounds conversational and authentic (and not just filled with incessant *you know's* and *uhm's*).

I work with students every year who have written boring, confusing essays, but once I get them to *talk* about themselves, they have brilliant things to say. I am constantly exhorting them to *"Write that down!"* They fail to realize that the way they naturally speak is often all they need.

PRO TIP: Want to know if your essay sounds right? Have someone read it out loud to you. You can even get your computer to read it to you if you are reluctant to have a human do it. Our eyes are terrible editors, but our ears can tell when something is wrong.

Draft Kings

Talking and outlining and planning is all well and good, but eventually you have to sit down and write.

And it is going to be terrible.

No one I have ever worked with has written a submittable essay on the first try. It's going to be a hodgepodge of good ideas lost in a morass of wordiness and vague generalities.

I have also read enough college essays to know that somewhere, deep within that dreadful first draft, is a phrase that will become the centerpiece of the whole essay. The trick is knowing how to find the nugget hiding among all that fool's gold.

When my older son first wrote his college essay about going on a Boy Scout campout, it was pretty dismal.

After I read it all, I asked him to find the one line in the whole essay that could not possibly have been written by anyone else applying to college that year. He identified a line near the end of the essay that described what it was like as a Den Chief being chased through the woods by a pack of young Cub Scouts. And he was right—that was the hook—and it became the beginning of the essay, not some random detail near the end of a bland linear storytelling exercise.

Once he knew how the essay should start, he had a clearer vision for how to tell his story.

So what kind of writer are you? Kurt Vonnegut once claimed there were two types, **swoopers** and **bashers**: "Swoopers write a story quickly, higgledy-piggledy, crinkum-crankum, any which way. Then they go over it again painstakingly, fixing everything that is just plain awful or doesn't work. Bashers go one sentence at a time, getting it exactly right before they go on to the next one. When they're done they're done."

No matter your process—and most high school students are swoopers—it's not going to be over quickly.

Fear is the Path to the Dark Side

Around the turn of the century, I bought a new iMac computer. When I got it home, I couldn't find the user's manual, so I called up the Apple Store. The employee told me that Apple products no longer came with printed directions, but I could go to their website and download it if I liked. I explained that if the computer isn't working, it's tough to get on the internet to read about troubleshooting. I have since realized that my dependence on antiquated user's manuals are antithetical to the millennial mindset. They do not want to read directions; they want to explore.

When it comes to the college essay, students should write with a sense of freedom, not foreboding. Let Jedi Master Yoda be your guide:

- "Do or do not. There is no try."
- "Fear is the path to the dark side. Fear leads to anger. Anger leads to hate. Hate leads to suffering."
- "Always pass on what you have learned."
- "Patience you must have, my young Padawan."

Don't Count Your Words Before They Are Written

We have established that it is unrealistic to read an entire book about how to write an essay, so here is some highly condensed, practical advice for polishing up essays so you can **retain your individuality while improving your readability.**

Paragraph the Heck out of It: Astonishingly, many applicants submit essays that are just one giant, rambling paragraph. Do not be that person. If a magazine article is published as one paragraph, people will instinctively skip it (*too long; didn't read*). The same goes for college essays and even the shorter supplemental essays. While there is no set number of paragraphs (please do not think it has to be a five-paragraph essay), six to eight is pretty good for a two-page essay. One student I worked with wrote a 350-word supplemental essay that was broken up into 11 paragraphs—and it was excellent.

And yes, you can have one-sentence paragraphs.

You can even have a one-word paragraph.

Really.

Every Word Counts (Literally): If the directions say the word count is 650, do not try to sneak in 651. In fact, admissions officers would probably appreciate it if you did not feel compelled to use every word at your disposal and could effectively say what needs to be said in 600 words, but do not come in with fewer than 500.

And let's be clear—you want all these words to count! Do not waste your precious opportunity to impress admissions officers with pointless prose.

Most of the time wordiness is easy to fix:

WORDY (15 words): I really enjoy riding my bike through the mountains in the middle of the night.

BETTER (5 words): I love midnight mountain biking.

LESSON: Long prepositional phrases are frequently tacked on to the end of a sentence and can often be cut or repurposed as adjectives before the noun. Avoid empty words like *really* and *very*.

* * *

WORDY (29): I have done many outside extracurricular activities in my life, but the one thing that has helped me grow the most as a person is the sport of volleyball.

BETTER (5): Volleyball gives me complete joy.

LESSON: Empty phrases that say nothing should be cut. When else would you have participated in these activities *but during your lifetime*? Would volleyball help you grow *as a penguin*?

* * *

WORDY (21): As my situation got worse and worse, I thought to myself, "How am I ever going to find my way home?"

BETTER (11): As my situation worsened, I wondered how I would get home.

LESSON: Avoid repetition. Could you really think to someone else? Do not quote your own thoughts or internal monologue.

* * *

WORDY (24): In the summer before my junior year of high school, I traveled to Las Vegas, Nevada, to save my uncle from a crazed bookie.

BETTER (11): Last summer I rescued my uncle from a crazed Vegas bookie.

LESSON: Because you are applying to be a college freshman, they know that your junior year was *in high school* (duh!). It's also known as "last summer." And for major cities with distinctive names (including New York, Boston, Dallas, Chicago, Los Angeles, Philadelphia, Seattle, New Orleans, Houston, and Miami), you do not need to include the state as well. If you are from Portland, Springfield, or Kansas City, then you should specify which one.

What's a Synonym for Thesaurus?

As far as teenage relationships go, a thesaurus can be your best friend and your worst enemy. Utilizing a thesaurus (who are we kidding, no one owns a thesaurus—you use the internet) is vital to avoid using the same key word repeatedly (incessantly, constantly, ad nauseam, ad infinitum) or to find a more exact (specific, precise, explicit) word.

Just because you learned a bunch of fancy words for the SAT does not mean you need to see how many you can cram into your essays. Even if that is the way you actually talk (be real, you don't), your reader will assume that you are just using the thesaurus—even if you are eschewing such bourgeois accoutrements.

A further word of caution on using the thesaurus: I get essays all the time that have some elevated language. I am usually willing to give students the benefit of the doubt, but once I reach a word that is used incorrectly by someone who has obviously just right-clicked on the word and picked out a grandiloquent surrogate, then I tend to doubt the veracity of all the other pseudointellectual words they deployed. Like my grandpappy used to say: Don't use a five-dollar word when a 25-cent one will do.

Grammer Errers

Nothing torpedoes an essay quicker than grammatical mistakes—the simpler, the more catastrophic. You can get away with a split infinitive (the MLA no longer prohibits them) or maybe even a comma splice, but do not confuse *it's* and *its* or use *whose* when you mean *who's*.

And do not butcher the name of the college (or call it a college when it's a university!). Referring to the school as *John* Hopkins, *Stamford* University, or the University of *South* California is a guaranteed disaster.

A few years ago at commencement, a local college president was brought in as our graduation speaker. He referred to my school by the wrong name at least three times in the first five minutes. It was like one of those Southwest Airlines commercials—you could almost hear the announcer ask, "Wanna get away?"

Parents, you can do your part by looking for these errors, but do not be pedantic about how many spaces go after end punctuation (old people were taught two spaces; today the MLA says just one, so deal with it, dad).

GET REAL: Most admissions officers are not English majors or strict grammarians—one misplaced comma does not mean you will get denied. There's a fine line between a harmless typo and gross error. I once had to reassure a panicked student that it was no big deal she had accidentally duplicated an entire phrase on her Common App essay. Harvard either did not notice or did not care—she got in Early.

Ruminations on Punctuation

Periods? Boring. Commas? They can, on occasion, clutter up your prose, or worse, cause you to ramble, all over the place. Here is a punctuation primer for picky people contemplating prose.

Commas: Comma errors make me crazy. If you do not know basic comma rules at this point, a highly selective college might not be the right place for you. That said, if you notice a lot of commas in your essay, your flow will be choppy and probably confusing. Be clear, be direct, and if you want to attend Oxford, then you should know how (and when) to use the Oxford comma. See what I did there?

Semicolons: The semicolon is the most intimidating punctuation mark because so few people know how to actually use it; fewer still can utilize it correctly. In school, I suggest that students try to include one semicolon per English essay; however, for college essays, I defer to the wisdom of Kurt Vonnegut: "Don't use semicolons! They are transvestite hermaphrodites, representing exactly nothing. All they do is suggest you might have gone to college." And since you are clearly not in college yet, why bother?

Quotation Marks: Try to avoid putting dialogue in your essay unless it's absolutely essential. You do not need to say that you told your friend, "thanks." If you want to show sarcasm or include an uncommon foreign word, use italics, not quotation marks. *Grazie!* And stay away from single quotes. For whatever 'reason,' students 'love' just 'randomly' using 'single' quotes, and they can never explain 'why' they do it. The only time to ever use single quotes is when you have a quote within a quote, and that should not happen in a college essay.

Ellipses: Unless you are using a long quotation, you probably will not need these, but if you do utilize a quote with words omitted in the middle, put brackets around the periods and your software should link them into one symbol. Example (from *Hamlet* via *The Simpsons*): "Brevity is [...] wit." Never begin or end a quotation with an ellipses—you can start or end a quote wherever you like—thus there is no need for ellipses.

Question Marks: Use sparingly—if at all. Your job is to inform colleges about you. Tell them a story. Do not ask questions, rhetorical or otherwise. Know what I mean?

Exclamation Marks: Amateurish! Do not shout! Do not gush! And absolutely, positively no doubling or tripling of exclamation points!!! Finally, do not ever ever ever use exclamation (or question) marks at the end of the first or last sentence of your essay! Sad!

PRO TIP: If you want to show emphasis, consider italicizing a word rather than dropping in an exclamation point. And do not use ALL CAPS because we all know THAT PERSON WHO EMAILS OR TEXTS IN ALL CAPS—and that person annoys us.

Parentheses: These are fantastic if you want to include an aside (you know, something non-essential but interesting) as you tell your story. Don't overdo it, but parentheses will allow you to drop in a bit of info with style.

Dashes: Ah, now here's the punctuation mark you should be using more often. Dashes have the functionality of commas and parentheses—but with greater impact. Just type two hyphens in a row—do not put spaces around them—and your computer will automatically turn the hyphens into a dash—presto! (For Google Docs you will need to insert the dash—look under Special Characters for the *em dash*.) Remember, all things in moderation—including moderation—but if you mix in some dashes and parentheses (pretty please), then your commas will not have to do all the work by themselves.

Don't Be a Noob

Language changes, albeit slowly. Sometimes a catalyst comes along like William Shakespeare to shake up the language by inventing new words that eventually become part of everyday speech (including *assassination, eyeball,* and *swagger*).

Thanks to social media, texting, and pop culture, new words are cropping up all the time, and many terms like *binge-watch, live-tweet,* and *humblebrag* make it into the mainstream vernacular seemingly overnight. And while these words probably will not cause you any grief if you put them in your application, some internet conventions will hurt your chances.

Do not drop in a hashtag (#YOLO) unless you are being ironic (more on humor in a bit), and avoid emojis and emoticons if you want to be taken seriously. ;)

I Put a Spell on You

This book was written originally in Google Docs, which is a wonderful invention and allows for speedy collaboration. Just before completing the final draft, everything was copied into a Word document, and there was so much red underlining. Turns out,

Google Docs missed a lot of rudimentary spelling errors. So be sure to run every written component of your application through Word, just to be safe.

Everyone has their pet peeves, but here are a few spelling mistakes that consistently raise the hackles of admissions professionals.

- **Everyday** is an adjective (an *everyday* problem). **Every day** is for everything else (I run five miles *every day*).
- If you want to be **a part of** a communal learning environment, then college is for you. If you want to be **apart** of such a place, that means you want to be far from it.
- For the most part, **affect** is a verb and **effect** is a noun.
- To think is to **wonder**; to roam is to **wander**.
- Use **number** if you can count something (the *number* of supplemental essays you will write for each college will vary). If you're discussing size, then use **amount** (the *amount* of writing might be more than expected).
- It's not the **honor role** (or **honors society**) and be careful if you attend an International **Baccalaureate** (not Bachelorette) school.
- If you are intrigued, then your interest has been **piqued** (not *peaked*).
- If you are not easily rattled, then you are **unfazed** (not *unphased*).
- You might be shocked how many students will say they are *intellegent* (which immediately calls into question their IQ). Other frequently misspelled words that threaten your legitimacy as a serious applicant: *definately* or *defiantly* (definitely), *independant* (independent) and *validictorian* (valedictorian) or *salutitorian* (salutatorian).
- Do not misspell the name of the university such as Columbia (not Colombia) or Indiana University (not India). Please make sure you know how to write the formal name of the school. It's Indiana University, not the University of Indiana, for instance.
- If you want to study *psycology, buisness, chemstriy* or *calclulus/calculas*, be sure to spell-check.
- If you are a varsity captain, do not call yourself a *varsity captian*.
- Your counselor will help you along the way (not your *counciler, councillor*, or *counsellor*). And that person who runs your public (not *pubic*) school is the principal (not *principle*).
- When using technical or medical terms, don't let autocorrect turn your essay about Asperger's syndrome into a story about *ass burgers*.
- Finally, you are in high school (not *highschool* or *High School*), and you are applying to college (not *collage*).

Show Don't Tell

Three little words are the cornerstone of your essay: **Show. Don't Tell.** Too many essays are full of vague references or glittering generalities that do not let us know much about you. Be specific. To wit:

TELL: I learned an important lesson that day.
SHOW: I learned to never trust a guy named Ace in a game of Three-Card Monte.

TELL: I have always been a good student.
SHOW: I made a B for the first time last year, and I could not have been prouder.

TELL: I want to attend Stanford.
SHOW: Stanford affords me the opportunity to study both petroleum engineering and computer science while continuing my work as an advocate for preserving the redwoods.

TELL: Whataburger is the greatest restaurant in the whole world. Nuff said.
SHOW: My love of the Honey Butter Chicken Sandwich is so steadfast that I am only applying to colleges that have a Whataburger within a 30-mile radius.

PRO TIP: Cut down on "to be" verbs and extraneous adjectives.

And while you are telling the colleges all about you, do not mention what the colleges already know, including information that is clearly on your transcript or on other parts of your application. And nix the obvious information about their college. They know when the college was founded and what city they are in.

And Now For Something Completely Different: Using Humor

In Arthur Miller's play *Death of a Salesman,* Willy Loman offers some job interviewing tips to his son Biff, which includes the advice, "don't crack any jokes." Willy understands that "everybody likes a kidder, but nobody lends him money."

People cite a sense of humor as one of the most important qualities for likability, but displaying your comedic skills in a college essay is, as W.C. Fields might say, fraught with peril.

Tone is so hard to read that even innocuous texts and emails have been misconstrued with calamitous results. A study published in the December 2005 *Journal of Personality and Social Psychology* showed that roughly half the participants could not determine if a sample email was serious or sarcastic.

Try not to take this the wrong way, kids, but what teenagers find funny is typically not going to go over well in the hallowed halls of ivy-covered buildings.

I have taught a senior English class about comedy, and one of the cornerstone lessons is to learn where to aim your humor. Most comedy, especially satire, is targeted at the rich and powerful. People enjoy the idea of taking the pompous and hypocritical elites down a notch (see Jonathan Swift's satirical masterpiece "A Modest Proposal").

The problem with "punching down" is that when you make fun of the poor and disadvantaged, it makes you look like a jerk.

If you aim at your own level, you poke fun at yourself or others like you. This is why Jerry Seinfeld was so incensed when his dentist, Tim Whatley (a pre-*Breaking Bad* Bryan Cranston), converted to Judaism just so he could tell Jewish jokes. The logic goes like this: Unless you are one of us, you cannot make jokes about us, so once you get accepted into one of these colleges, *then* you can start cracking wise.

In *Animal House* (loosely based on shenanigans at Dartmouth), two members of Delta House, Boon and Otter, witness ROTC Col. Douglas C. Neidermeyer verbally abusing one of their pledges. Otter says, "He can't do that to our pledges," to which Boon adds, "Only we can do that to our pledges."

So you see the problem with using comedy. Aim high, and you are probably making fun of the very colleges to which you are applying. The rich, the powerful, the educated—those are some of your future classmates. Sure you can try to make fun of the Harvard-educated Texan who couldn't decide which detail to mention first. Or you could ask, "How many Columbia students does it take to change a lightbulb?" (Answer: 76. One to change the lightbulb, 50 to protest the light bulb's right not to change, and 25 to hold a counter-protest), but when it comes to comedy, proceed with caution.

And do not even think of bringing political humor into the mix. Barack Obama, Hillary Clinton, George W. Bush, Ted Cruz, Carly Fiorina, Ben Carson, Bobby Jindal and Donald Trump all received a bachelor's or advanced degree from an Ivy League school, and others like Bernie Sanders (University of Chicago) went to an Ultra as well.

Making fun of oneself is somewhat safer, but if you are careless, you might cast yourself in a negative light. As long as you are reasonably self-effacing about minor things, you can find fault with yourself, but avoid venturing into darker territory.

Details, Details (What to Leave In, What to Leave Out)

The best essays are full of specific, descriptive language. This does not mean they are flowery, overstuffed, or rambling. There needs to be specificity so readers can see that you pay attention to the world around you and that you have the vocabulary and writing skills to express yourself clearly.

But sometimes, in the attempt to fill an essay with details, there are some specifics that should probably be left unsaid because such details are so tone deaf that it makes the student seem sheltered, naïve, or outright intolerant.

DULL: I spent the entire trip to New York doing homework.

TOO MUCH INFORMATION: I spent the entire flight to NYC on my family's Gulfstream working with my personal tutor on my physics project.

JUST RIGHT: On the red-eye flight to New York, I spent all night trying to perfect my proposal for a fully functional lunar base.

* * *

DULL: I made some great friends during my summer in Prague.

TMI: I became best friends in Prague with a guy covered in satanic tattoos—it just goes to show that you can't always judge a book by its cover.

JUST RIGHT: Even though I initially disliked Karl for having so many tattoos, we became inseparable during my summer in Prague.

Basically, anything that makes you sound like a spoiled, rich (probably white) child of privilege who lives in a big house, drives a nice car, and attends a top private school, should be downplayed.

In 2015, an essay by University of Michigan student Jesse Klein in *The Michigan Daily* went viral. Klein began the essay ("Relative wealth") by stating that her "family's household income is $250,000 a year, but I promise you I am middle class. I live in a $2 million dollar house, but I promise you I am still middle class."

The essay was a sincere attempt to discuss the differences between middle and upper class life she experienced in Ann Arbor, Michigan, and her home in Silicon Valley, but the internet did not take kindly to her definition of middle class.

You might think you are being brave, even noble, by discussing subjects like race relations, LGBTQ+ rights, economics, religion, or politics. And while these topics can show how thoughtful you are, it is important to have someone outside your peer group evaluate your essay before you submit.

Your college counselor or a trusted teacher should be capable of steering you away from essays that make you sound prejudiced or ignorant (neither of which colleges are looking for).

And what's inappropriate? With apologies to Jeff Foxworthy...

- If you write about how your housekeeper is like a member of the family...you might get denied.
- If you write about how your show horse is your best friend...you might get denied.
- If you talk about how the hotel in Paris didn't have Wi-Fi...you might get denied.
- If you say that you couldn't fit your golf clubs into the trunk of your BMW i8...you might get denied.
- If you write about how your elite private school is diverse because they let in some of the faculty member's kids...you might get denied.

A final word, from high atop a soapbox: Let's have a moratorium on complaining that you are under so much pressure applying to college. It's not like your only options are Yale or jail. Getting into a top college is high drama manufactured by academia, the media (especially U.S. News & World Report), your parents, your friends, and probably you, too.

GET REAL: Pressure is not whether or not you get into Princeton. Pressure is bussing tables every day until midnight in order to make enough money to ensure that your family isn't evicted from their cramped apartment.

If you think for even a minute that you have a legitimate chance of getting into a highly selective college, then you probably will, but you will be just as happy and successful if you attend a school that does not have a single-digit acceptance rate, so dial it down a notch.

PERKS AND RECS

Why So Many Recommendation Letters Are a Joke

CHAPTER 9

It's not really work,
It's just the power to charm.

— *David Bowie, "Modern Love"*

THE TEACHER RECOMMENDATION LETTER just might be the most nebulous variable in the admissions equation.

Students know their grade point average, test scores, and what is on their résumé. They wrote their essays, and they were present for the interviews. But the teacher rec is a real crapshoot. And often it's just crap.

In an era when some high schools are moving away from issuing class rank and grade inflation is becoming so rampant that it can all but render GPA meaningless, there are precious few ways for colleges to discover what a student is *really* like— especially in the classroom. And for the Ultras, it goes without saying that an applicant's grades and test scores should be strong. Essays allow students to tell their own stories, and interviews give a sense of their personalities, but the teacher rec should ideally give an *objective* view of what the student brings to the classroom experience even though it is, in essence, *subjective*.

As an English teacher who has taught mostly juniors and seniors over the years, I have written hundreds of rec letters, and I always assumed that my fellow educators did their due diligence when it came to writing their letters.

And then it was time for my first son to apply to college.

At the end of his junior year, Zach's math teacher had sent us an unsolicited email in which she said nothing but positive things about him, so he made sure to ask her to write one of his recommendation letters.

One month before his Early Decision application deadline, his math teacher forwarded a copy of the rec letter she had written for him. Here it is, in its entirety:

To whom it may concern:

I highly recommend Zach for admissions to your esteemed university. Zach took PreCalculus from me during the 2013-14 school year. PreCalculus is an honors course and Zach earned above a 95 for both semesters. In addition he showed strong leadership skills during his daily work assignments in class. He helped others in the classroom and proved to be a diplomatic and charismatic in his leadership style. I remember one class where nobody in his group understood how to solve a complex trigonometric problem. Zach thought about it for a while and then came up with a strategy to solve that problem that he shared with his peers. Other members of his group would chime in and, together, they were the first group to finish the problem. Zach is definitely college material.

I believe that Zach would be an excellent asset to your university. Thank you for considering his application.

There are a multitude of problems with this teacher's letter. For starters, it's basically one paragraph full of bland statements, and it mentions grades that are already on the transcript. Then there are the vague recollections that sound like they could describe practically any student. And if you think it reads like a form letter—you are correct, it is! She told us that it was a "generic" letter, but she asked us to let her know if he needed something more.

Heck yeah students need something more!

This was not a rookie teacher, mind you, yet she wrote such a terse, tepid letter that I knew it would not help his cause getting into an engineering program at the most competitive schools in the country.

I emailed her and politely thanked her for sharing the letter (it's definitely *not* standard operating procedure for teachers to share rec letters with students). I mentioned that, as a fellow teacher who once taught at her school, I appreciated all her efforts. I then mentioned some of the schools where my son was applying so she would understand the level of competition he faced. Finally, I took her up on her offer to write a more personalized letter.

She said that she would draft another version, and that was the last we heard from her. We never saw the revised letter—if there ever was one.

My son's other rec letter was written by his junior-year English teacher. Amazingly, the English teacher also shared his rec letter with us—completely unsolicited—and he finished his letter weeks before the math teacher. Zach had requested the letters before school started because some teachers prefer to get recs done over the summer while others write them whenever they have time throughout the fall.

Even though my son was not planning to be a liberal arts major, the English teacher's letter was a whole page (with multiple paragraphs!), and it was full of warmth and highly specific anecdotes. It gave a sense of what kind of person he was— not just what his grades were. Reading the English rec made the math teacher's letter all the more galling because it looked even worse in comparison.

Did the math teacher's letter hurt his chances? Probably not. After all, roughly 80 percent of admissions decisions are based on grades, curriculum, and testing. But it certainly didn't help.

GET REAL: The more exclusive the college, the more important the rec letters, but even then, few schools consider the rec letter an important part of the decision-making process (only 15 percent in 2014 according to NACAC, down from 20 percent in 2006).

Thanksgiving Traditions

Every family has its own Thanksgiving rituals. My wife and I are from the same hometown, so each year we would pack up the kids and drive back to play in the annual Turkey Bowl flag football game followed by the traditional holiday meal. And everyone would stay for the weekend—everyone but me.

My extended holiday tradition involved driving back home after my tryptophan overload and sequestering myself in my office for the rest of the weekend to write college rec letters.

This was the late 1990s, and most of my students were applying Regular Decision. Furthermore, applications were still done with self-addressed envelopes, fill-in-the-blank teacher evaluation forms, and individualized letters for each university.

Those days I was at a large public high school (the same one that both my children eventually attended), and I taught about 190 seniors each year (five or six senior English classes—minimum 35 kids per class). I wound up writing rec letters for nearly a third of them—on average half a dozen letters per student.

I would fill out by hand the student assessment form (including short-answer questions), then I would write a letter for every college. I would compose a one-page letter to, let's say, Sewanee, then print it out, sign it, stuff the envelope, and seal it (I invested in one of those water dabbers because there are only so many envelopes a person can lick). And if students forgot to affix correct (or any) postage, I covered that, too.

I repeated the process, modifying the letter as needed, depending on the college (because I believed in the personal touch). If students were applying to my alma mater, I mentioned in the letter why I thought they would be a good fit. And if I knew something specific about other schools, I mentioned that as well.

The process alternated between thrilling (finding ways to impart to schools just how special some of these students were) and mind-numbing (did I load the letterhead in the printer upside down again?).

My old school did not have a system to regulate the number of rec letters a teacher would write, and I never turned anyone away. It was a deal I made with every student at the beginning of the year: I do not care what you have done in the past—if you work hard for me this semester, I will write your rec letter. Most students earned that letter.

When I was just starting out, I had the good fortune to have some phenomenal colleagues who would share sample rec letters with me and offer feedback on mine. I never received any assistance from the school counselors—assisting teachers on college matters was not their job. Writing rec letters was (and still is) a largely unregulated task with little or no oversight.

This should not come as a shock, but the quality of rec letters varies wildly, even in the best of high schools. Being a great calculus, physics, government, Latin, or English teacher does not guarantee that those teachers have the time, inclination, or ability to write effective rec letters.

I have known many impressive colleagues over the decades, but not all of them embraced the art of epistolary discourse. Most of the time a high school does not care if the chemistry teacher writes well. Or if the baseball coach is a talented wordsmith. Or if the economics teacher frequently has trouble with subject-verb agreement.

The rules of the game dictate that students never see their rec letters (unless the teachers decide to share).

On every teacher rec form there is a box to check that states whether or not the student waives the right to see the rec letters before they are sent, and no one ever reserves the right to see the letters.

PRO TIP: Always waive your right to see teacher rec letters. If you have any doubt that your teacher will say nice things, then ask another teacher. If you do not waive your right, it indicates that you might not trust the teacher or you have something to hide that you fear the teacher might mention. You have every right to be curious, even anxious, about what they will say, but it's not worth the risk. Ideally teachers will write about you on your best day, so let that provide some peace of mind.

I Came in Like a Rec-ing Ball

If you think that students from large public schools are at a disadvantage when it comes to rec letters, you are right.

When I made the transition from full-service public school to elite private school at the turn of the century, I soon discovered what some of that tuition money was paying for—college counselors.

There was an entire department of professionals whose prime directive was to work with students and parents on getting their kids into the best colleges. And the expectation was that 100 percent of our students were going to college. About half of our students would wind up attending Ultras each year, but then again, we have had years when almost half the senior class were named National Merit Finalists, so it stands to reason.

It has been established that family income is the primary factor in determining who does best on standardized tests and gets into the most exclusive colleges. The chasm between well-funded schools and poorer campuses is even more noticeable when it comes to college counseling.

Consider the facts: The average public high school counselors spend just 22 percent of their time on college counseling, while the average private school counselors devote about 55 percent of the time to college issues.

According to the American School Counselor Association, the recommended student-to-counselor ratio is 250-to-1, but only two states, Vermont and Wyoming, met or exceeded that level of coverage. In 2017, the ASCA revealed that the national average student-to-counselor ratio was actually 482-to-1 (based on the 2014-2015 school year). The worst ratios were found in Arizona (924-to-1), California (760-to-1), and Michigan (729-to-1)

Across the country, there are almost 850,000 high school students who have no access to any counselors at all. In one 2016 investigation, the *Houston Press* reported that 28 Houston high schools didn't have a single counselor or college advisor, so in HISD, the student-to-counselor ratio was really more like 1,800:1.

At private schools, the ratio is closer to 30:1.

The disparity between public and private schools in terms of writing effective rec letters was highlighted in 2015 when the University of California at Berkeley began requiring rec letters for the first time (one teacher rec and one letter from somebody who knows the applicant well). This made Berkeley the first school in the UC system to require rec letters. Many selective colleges require two teacher rec letters. While not all large state schools require rec letters, the most selective state flagships schools require one or two recs.

Critics point out that by requiring rec letters, Cal and other schools will perpetuate disadvantage by rewarding students from affluent schools whose teachers and counselors are more adept at playing the college admissions game and knowing what kind of letters to write. And they are correct.

GET REAL: Admissions officers are keenly aware that not every counselor has the time or resources to write a letter of recommendation. Colleges ask counselors how many students are in their caseload. If the counselor has over 100, the admissions office understands why a counselor cannot write a full letter for each (or any) student. However, if the counselor has 35 students, then the letters are expected to contain more information.

When I started working at a private school, college counselors would teach one class and then work on their other duties. And then that wasn't enough, so college counselors, who were some of the best teachers, were pulled from the classroom to work exclusively on college readiness.

Even with that much personalized attention, a significant number of families pay additional big bucks to independent education consultants to assist in the process. I have worked with many seniors on their applications (either in class, outside of school, or *pro bono*), but my modest fees are nothing compared to some companies (and individuals) that charge $20,000, $40,000 or even $100,000 (for the deluxe package) in order to give students a leg up in the process.

GET REAL: Families with the means to hire independent education consultants (i.e., "private counselors") are often less likely to need them since their kids tend to be enrolled in high schools with excellent in-house counselors. If the outside counselor does not know what they are doing, it can actually harm the student. For example, a parent who hangs out a shingle because their child got into an Ultra is no expert, and they might give advice that conflicts with the experienced in-house counselor.

The one thing that all those college counselors and paid consultants cannot do is write the teacher recommendation letter. This book is not intended as a how-to guide for high school teachers or counselors on writing effective rec letters. There are excellent videos and slideshow presentations from colleges on the web that provide all the information they need.

Students should read this section in order to understand what the teachers are going to write about and then be sure to display the kind of behavior that will make it easier for teachers to write wonderful things about them that the colleges will value.

Spoiler alert: Making good grades is just the start.

In brief, a rec letter for the Ultras needs to show more than what is stated on the transcript. Colleges want to know what will be the "value added" quantity of the student. Teachers know that it takes more than strong grades to be considered a phenomenal student. They should ask themselves:

- Does the student participate actively or just when called upon?
- Does the student use incisiveness to contribute to class discussions or by having distracting discussions with their friends?
- Does the student work well with others?
- Is the student a ruthless mercenary—only focused on grades—or do they display a genuine love of learning?
- Did the student display exceptional effort to succeed on an assignment?
- Does the student display grit?
- How does the student accept criticism?
- How mature is the student?
- Is this student creative—and how did it manifest itself in class?
- Has this student made a positive impact on your class?
- Is this student honorable?
- What makes this student different?

A Note to Teachers: It's Not About You

Too often the teacher rec letter winds up being more about the teacher than the student. You do not need to mention too much about yourself, but you should state up-front what your relationship is with the student and what your course entails, but check yourself before you write something unfounded like "my course is the hardest in the school." If you have been teaching for decades, and this is one of your finest students ever, then mentioning your tenure is germane to the letter, but if you are a second-year teacher, you should probably keep that to yourself.

Just like students writing their college essays, teachers also need to remember to "Show. Don't Tell." If the student is innovative or determined or brilliant, then teachers would be wise to cite specific examples that demonstrate these qualities. Resist the temptation to talk about what is already on the transcript or what they do in other realms of the school. If you are the math teacher, do not spend a lot of time discussing the student's volleyball skills or violin prowess. Colleges want to know about performance *in your realm*, so unless you are also the volleyball coach or orchestra instructor, keep the extraneous information to a minimum.

The transcript most certainly *does not* speak for itself, so it is incumbent on you to shed light on the situation by describing the student accurately, documenting what makes them special, and providing enough detail so colleges get a true sense of what the student is like.

Sometimes teachers get a little too effusive with praise and wind up peppering their recs with purple prose. Resist the temptation to overstate the case. And try to keep the letters to one page. These kids are 17 years old, not Nobel Laureates—a single page is fine.

But the worst thing a teacher can do is often quite common—teachers recycle the same letter year after year for multiple students. You cannot expect teachers to avoid repeating some stock phrases (there are only so many ways to say someone is talented), but when a teacher does nothing but change the name on a letter, it is a dereliction of duty, and the colleges do notice.

True story: A college admissions director once told me about a time that their college received the exact same student rec letter from two different teachers! After some initial confusion, the college did a little investigating, and it turned out that a veteran teacher had shared a sample rec letter with a younger colleague in another department to show him how they were written, and the young teacher had been using the letter verbatim. When both teachers were asked to write a letter for the same student, the young teacher was busted.

Help Me Help You

Those sage words from sports agent Jerry Maguire to his only remaining client, Arizona Cardinals wide receiver Rod Tidwell, are apt when it comes to teacher rec letters: Help them help you. Students do not fully appreciate how much they can assist the teachers with the rec letters, and thus, by the transitive property of self-promotion, benefit themselves.

The first thing students need to realize is that colleges generally expect letters from teachers in different fields. And that does not mean one English teacher and one history teacher. Colleges prefer one math/science teacher and one liberal arts teacher, so whether you are a "math girl" or a "history boy" you need to do well enough in at least two classes to have confidence that these teachers will write for you. That said, if you have fantastic grades in math and science and good grades in English and history, it would be advisable to ask both your STEM teachers to write your recs.

Colleges want to hear from your most recent teachers—the ones from junior year or *maybe* sophomore year. **Unfortunately, many rising seniors realize too late that they should have been forging positive relationships with their teachers, not antagonizing them in the classroom or pestering them about when they are going to return a test or essay.**

You might be setting the world on fire at the start of your senior year, but that is usually not enough of a track record to go on; however, as long as you are not applying early—and you have done exceptionally well in a highly advanced class like Calculus or AP English—then you could ask one of your senior teachers to write you a rec in December (which is not a lot of advance notice, so you had better be doing some amazing work). Similarly, you might have done an outstanding job as a freshman, but you should probably forget about asking your ninth grade teachers.

GET REAL: Sometimes it's just not possible to have a junior-year teacher write a rec letter. Maybe your teacher missed time because she went on maternity or medical leave, so she does not know you very well. Maybe your teacher retired and is living off the grid. Perhaps they left the school under acrimonious circumstances and might not be willing to write a letter. Maybe your family moved and you began school in the middle of your junior year. If there are mitigating circumstances that may cause you to solicit rec letters from anyone other than your junior-year teachers, make sure you explain this in your application—your counselor can also address it in his or her letter, which is another integral part of your file.

In the best of all worlds, you will have at least one teacher who has worked with you for multiple years in a variety of settings and knows you well. Maybe your advisor/homeroom teacher was also your track coach and AP US History teacher. Perhaps you have been on the yearbook for several years and the adviser was also your

AP English Language teacher. These are no-brainers as far as rec letters go. But not everyone forges a meaningful relationship with a teacher that spans several years.

What students frequently realize is that in the metaphorical race to college, like Pink Floyd once sang, students "missed the starting gun." While it is nice to make good grades, if you never raise your hand in class, come in to discuss papers, or pay attention to lectures, then it is unlikely that your teacher will have much to work with besides the grades. Just as Laurel Thatcher Ulrich observed in 1976 that "well-behaved women seldom make history," it is also true that quiet honors students who do not participate in class will seldom receive the most glowing rec letters.

On the other end of the spectrum, if you burn too many bridges, then you may find yourself desperately racking your brain to find a teacher—any teacher—who will write you a letter. Loud, obnoxious students who distract the class and prevent anyone else from chiming in will not endear themselves.

And if you fancy yourself a comedian, just remember that there is a fine line between class clown and village idiot.

When colleges receive a weak or non-flattering letter from a teacher, they may wonder about your performance or question your judgment since you could not secure a letter from a teacher who would say something nicer about you.

Remembrance of Things Past

Some high schools require students to complete a self-survey regarding the classroom experience. These reflections are invaluable tools for the teachers writing the rec letters. Teachers know what they taught and what grades the student made, but they do not usually know what the students got out of a class—unless they are told.

If there is no self-survey form in your school, then you should absolutely create one for yourself. Students should complete the information thoroughly and thoughtfully—and always typed. Your teachers can observe your performance in class, but unless you talk frequently with your teacher outside the classroom, they have no way of knowing just what the class *meant* to you. So make sure you address the following:

- What was your proudest moment in the class? (not necessarily your best grade)
- What obstacles or challenges did you overcome in this class?
- What was your favorite lesson/unit/assignment/book?
- What colleges are you applying to and what do you want to study?
- How did this class prepare you for your intended major?

The more your teacher knows about you *as a person* and your *educational goals*, the more likely they will write you an impressive rec letter.

So, if you are a good student who is reticent in class, hates to do group work, whines about every grade, and complains about how unfair or ridiculous the assignments are, you might not get the letter you need.

"BIRTHDAY?"
"NO, REC LETTER SEASON"

D.I.Y.

Teachers occasionally ask students to take a do-it-yourself approach with rec letters. This role-playing exercise can help the student understand what the teacher is looking for while also affording the student an opportunity to discuss the personal qualities that they think the college should know about. Would a teacher actually submit verbatim a rec letter written by a student? It's possible—especially if the letter is truthful and well written—which makes it all the more important to take the task seriously.

Do not be shocked if a teacher (or future employer) ever asks you to write your own rec letter. In large schools and companies, it is sometimes not feasible for teachers or bosses to know everything that you do to make yourself successful.

Back when my first book was released, I asked my publisher who writes the "About the Author" blurb that goes on the back of the book. He said, "You do."

While a bit disorienting at first, writing about oneself in third person is a useful technique, one that I have replicated for theater programs, course descriptions, and conference speaker profiles. Some creative writing teachers even have an exercise in which they assign students to write their own obituary—talk about forcing students to look ahead!

PRO TIP: Write a note to all your teachers at the end of junior year (or at the very least the ones that will—or might—write your rec letters). If you are going to ask them to write a letter for you, at least you will have already written one for them. Quid pro quo!

This Is How We Do It

Gone are the days of individualized rec letters for every college. In fact, gone are paper letters altogether. Today, most high schools use an online system like Naviance that uploads each rec letter and sends them to the applicant's colleges.

While this modern system definitely saves the teachers and counselors oodles of time, Naviance has been known to revamp their entire system without warning, which can lead to aggravation, confusion and delays. If you are facing a deadline and your school is still resolving Naviance issues, be prepared to give your teachers a pre-addressed, stamped envelope and ask them to send in a hard copy of the letter.

Uploading one form letter to Naviance prevents teachers from making specific comments to a particular college. So, for example, a teacher who graduated from Northwestern cannot mention that in the letter.

While I can no longer state in my letter that I used to roam the hallowed halls of Harvard (while I was working at an army-navy store in Cambridge while my wife was completing her final year of law school) or wax nostalgic about my alma mater where one of my students is now applying, the new uploading system definitely lightens the load, and I no longer worry about the letter getting lost in the mail.

GET REAL: I once worked with a tremendous friend and wonderful teacher who really loved to mention in rec letters that he was an alumnus of his alma mater (he would also have to send the letter to places besides his alma mater). His quite understandable thinking was that if he mentioned his alumnus status, it would carry extra weight. The truth is that unless he has serious connections and affiliations with the university, it does not add much.

I'll Make Him an Offer He Can't Refuse

Do teachers ever refuse to write rec letters?

Yes, they do.

The main reason you will get turned down is that the teacher is in high demand and simply does not have the time. Schools do not pay teachers to write these letters, so having them hand-craft these artisanal rec letters, which usually take at least an hour to write, comes at the expense of their personal and professional time—and there is only so much of that to go around.

Of course, a teacher might not want to write a letter for a student because, ethically, they do not think they can honestly evaluate the student without revealing details that would probably hurt the student's chances. In this situation, teachers will often fall back on the excuse that they simply have too many letters to write, so the student should ask someone else.

Some schools have a system in which students rank the teachers they would like to have write their rec letters, and the counselors come up with a list that divvies up the task more equitably. In these schools, teachers can alert the counselors if writing a letter for a particular student would be problematic.

In the absence of such a system, some teachers do far more than their fair share of rec letter writing than some of their colleagues (freshmen teachers are rarely overburdened with rec letter requests). So do not wait until the last minute to request a letter, and if a teacher turns down your request, then you need to look elsewhere.

PRO TIP: If your school does not have a system in place for students to request rec letters, then you should ask your teachers at the end of your junior year (or over the summer at the latest). This has two benefits: It shows you are responsible and organized enough to get the request in early, and it is somewhat flattering that you are entrusting them to help you get into college. If you are applying EA/ED to a school with rolling admissions, then state this explicitly to your teachers and ask if they can send the letter ASAP, otherwise they might wait until November.

There are lots of students who simply do not hit it off with a particular teacher (or vice versa), and most of the time these are not the teachers that you will ask for a rec letter.

I once had a bright student who was such a grade grubber that it would have clouded my letter—if the student had asked me for one—which, thankfully, she did not. There was no love of learning from this student, just an insatiable desire to get the highest grade. Once, near the beginning of the year, she came in to discuss a B+ paper, and she clearly was not listening to any of my suggestions on how to become a better writer—she was just there to fight for those two extra points. I finally asked her, "So, if I had marked your paper with all the same comments and suggestions, but had given you a 90 instead of an 88, would we be having this conversation?"

"No," was her matter-of-fact reply.

And while I never would have mentioned that exchange in a rec letter, this is the kind of student who will not get my very best effort.

The Scarlet Rec Letter

Would a teacher ever intentionally try to sabotage a student in a rec letter?

This question was posed to counselors across the country, both in high school and college, which resulted in some shocking, albeit atypical, stories.

In New York, one teacher actually approached a student and asked to write her rec letter, which she agreed to since he was her favorite teacher. In the letter, the teacher said that the student would not contribute much to a college. When the astonished college admissions office contacted the high school to see why the letter was so negative, they discovered that the teacher had written negatively about five other students. The teacher was put on leave and eventually left the school.

In 2001, a teacher wrote a two-page rec for a female student that said, among other things, "she supports the terrorists' actions—but her brothers were great."

Another teacher, clearly tired of being hounded by the student's mother, wrote, "If persistence is hereditary, he may do well in your program."

As one colleague noted, when schools receive letters like these, as infrequent as they are, "they're the kiss of death."

And sometimes things just get weird.

Years ago, one of my colleagues, a sophomore English teacher, was embroiled in a lawsuit filed by a litigious parent of a troubled student. They sued the teacher because their son earned a grade lower than they thought he deserved. When the ordeal was over, she was exonerated, but not without deep emotional and financial cost, and then the student had the temerity to ask her for a college rec letter! Sensing a trap (if she refused, would they sue her again?), she had to consult her lawyer to see if she could refuse the request. She could and she did.

I have only turned down one student request for a rec letter, and that was because the student was a habitual cheater. It took some asking, but he finally secured letters from two sophomore teachers who were unaware of his pathological dishonesty.

Ultimately, colleges notice when teachers damn the students with faint praise. Still, even for the mediocre or weak students, if a teacher agrees to write a letter, they tend to focus on the positive attributes of the applicant (it is, after all, a *recommendation* letter, not a *trash the applicant* letter). Sometimes teachers will put in more effort for the weaker students, especially if they are particularly amiable and inquisitive.

What teachers tend to do with the more problematic students, rather than focus on the negative, is to mix in some subtle words that indicate to the college that this is not a top student (as if the transcript didn't already paint that picture). Teachers say things like the student *could* be successful at college, not that the student undoubtedly will do well at the next level.

Sometimes there are teachers who will not write a great letter for particular students but are afraid to turn them down. This is an unfortunate situation, but these students will likely just get a basic letter.

The key is to get to know your teachers as soon as possible and make sure they know everything about you so they can write the best letter possible.

A Broader View: The Counselor Letter

Also required by many colleges is the counselor letter. In affluent schools, this is one of the primary functions of the college counseling department. Counselors meet frequently with the student, parents, and the faculty to learn everything they can about the student. Furthermore, they observe the student for years on campus in a variety of settings. By the time they have to write the counselor letter, they have a lot of material with which to work.

The counselor letter from a cash-strapped school is likely going to be a lot more formulaic because of time constraints. Counselors have hundreds of students for whom they rarely (if ever) meet with regarding college, so they cannot possibly know all their students well. You can try to help them by thoroughly filling out counselor questionnaires (or whatever form your school requires). Colleges understand the limitations placed on counselors, so you should not worry about the relative quality of generic counselor letters, but it is fair to point out that schools with a high-powered college counseling staff will provide universities with far more material than their counterparts. Much like the teacher rec letter, the importance of the counselor letter has been on the decline in the past decade, dropping from 21 percent of colleges treating them as "considerably important" in 2006 to 17 percent in 2014.

PRO TIP: If you attend a public school and your counselor changes before your senior year (kids get reshuffled all the time), you can still ask your previous counselor, who probably knows you better, to write your letter.

The counselor letter differs from the teacher rec because it offers not only specifics about the student, but **it puts that student's performance into context.** While a teacher might gush over a student's brilliance in a particular class, the counselor will have a more global perspective about the student and let the colleges know where the applicant ranks compared to all the students at that school. Counselor letters can also help explain any mitigating circumstances or grade outliers while also examining what makes the student stand out.

Good Counselors Know the Answers, Great Counselors Know the Questions

When I write my counselor letter, I write in a way that advocates for the student with a healthy dose of humor, hokeyness, and help. I see my letter as a means to make my arguments for admission as if I were the admissions officer.

After going through committee for hours, you get better at anticipating what the other committee members are going to question. In preparation, I try to address any of those possible issues in my rec letter. In essence, I use the counselor letter as a means of communicating admissions arguments.

GET REAL: Many parents ask counselors to call up the admissions office on behalf of their child to, you know, "advocate." Often, this is prefaced by "my friend said it was highly effective when the counselor called." This request seems to make sense except that most counselors want every student to get in everywhere they apply—not just one student. Unless a counselor is going to call every college for every student, it is unfair to ask them to make these calls on behalf of your student. The counselor letter is their advocacy, please don't ask for more.

Pulling out the Big Guns

Some colleges allow for supplemental rec letters. Check with the college to make sure of their policy.

If you have dedicated yourself to a particular activity at school and you know that there is a faculty member who will write you a killer rec, then by all means, ask. As a newspaper adviser, I always offer to write a supplemental letter for my editors. Students should only ask for additional recs if they think the teacher or coach will be able to shed light on the student's abilities and potential that the other teachers would not. The qualities I see in the newsroom are more about leadership, organization, and dedication than about being a good writer, so I have something to add that their science teacher, or even their English teacher, probably does not know.

Some students may wish to call upon individuals who are not classroom teachers. These tend to fall into two categories: adults who know the student beyond the classroom and high-powered alumni who are friends with the family of the applicant.

In the first case, if you have a job, you could have your boss write a letter. Or if you are a top athlete, the coach would be a natural fit. Maybe you participate in an elite dance troupe, youth choir, or theater group. Having the director write a letter would seem beneficial. Ditto for Scout leaders, especially for students who earned Gold Award or Eagle Scout.

It certainly would not hurt if you have a famous, powerful, or wealthy family friend who is an alumnae, faculty member, or member of the Board of Trustees. But you should know that if this person does not actually know *you*, then you probably will not get much of a bump. If the adult can speak about you with specificity, then you have a case, but if they only met you once when you were nine years old, then the letter will reek of your parents calling in a favor.

SUBURBAN LEGEND: Inside Man

We know a friend/colleague/relative/ neighbor who attended that college! If they write a rec letter, it will surely help!

Actually, probably not. Families enquire about this all the time, as if college admissions decisions were akin to getting a reference letter to join a country club. A high-powered, influential alumnus may very well help, but few families actually know anyone like that (although many alumni like to think they are).

There was one reported case in which a highly sought-after businessman was frequently called upon to write letters for his wealthy friends. The CEO used a code when writing the letters—if he referred to the student by their first names, that meant he actually knew them and endorsed their candidacy, but if the letter referred to the student with a title and last name (Mr. Milhouse or Miss Crabapple), that meant he knew little or nothing about the student.

All Together Now

As a teacher and a writer, I am sometimes dismayed when rec letters are the only kind of writing I have time to do. They are doubly strange because the person I am writing about will likely never see the letter. Meanwhile, complete strangers will evaluate my writing to help them make an admissions decision.

When I encounter a student who has enriched my life, and I get the chance to share their story with others, that's one of the best parts of the job.

At the end of this chapter is a letter I once wrote for a remarkable student. Every time I read it, I am reminded of a special student, the first Harvard student to graduate with a concentration in pre-med and Visual and Environmental Studies in many years. Today, she is in medical school and on her way to becoming a doctor who will one day help kids like her who were born with congenital birth defects.

Along the way, she made new friends, followed her passions, and branched out in ways that seemed impossible just a few years ago. Teachers get inspired to write letters for all kinds of students, not just the ones with the best grades, but getting teachers to write an effective letter on your behalf requires a lot more than just asking.

Dear Admissions Officer,

I am pleased to write this recommendation letter on Elaine's behalf. I had the privilege of teaching her in English III, and she is the illustrator of our school newspaper, which I advise. I've written innumerable college letters over the years for some impressive students, but Elaine's accomplishments are so remarkable that I must begin by saying that of all the seniors I know, she is most deserving of admission.

As a junior, Elaine stood out from a stellar crop of students—everything she did had an added element that set her apart. Her writing acumen is far beyond her peers, and her spring synthesis paper on the disenchantment of counterculture and the Beat Generation was easily the best I read. Little did I know that when the year started, Elaine didn't think much of English or her own power as a writer.

In the first semester, I was reading aloud excerpts from papers on *The Age of Innocence* to exemplify the usual good, bad and ugly aspects of their writing. When I read a stellar excerpt from Elaine's paper, anonymously, she took it correctly as an indication that she might be better at writing than she, or anyone, had given her credit.

Most people associate Elaine with her skill for painting and dance. I noticed her work when she was a freshman—looking at big displays of student art, one could not help but notice that her work was extraordinary. Right then I resolved to create a position of staff illustrator for the school paper, just for her. Fortunately, she agreed.

And then there is her ability to overcome adversity. I won't relate all of her surgeries or her struggle to achieve a sense of normalcy with a facial deformity. All I know is that one of the most talented students I've ever taught would almost never speak.

That's the background for the shocking decision that Elaine made—she ran for prefect at the end of last year. In her touching, funny and brilliant speech, I heard her say more than she had for an entire semester. Almost overnight, people who never knew she existed not only got to know her, but liked her, elected her, and wanted to hear more of what she had to say. It was as transformative a moment as I've ever seen.

As an English teacher, sometimes I opine that everyone doesn't get to see the true beauty and brilliance that some students can display through their writing. Like Thomas Gray once wrote, "Full many a flower is born to blush unseen and waste its sweetness on the desert air." Elaine, however, didn't wither away. Yes, she overcame a multitude of obstacles by excelling in art and academics, but more than that, she did what all of us wish to do but so rarely attempt—she did the thing that scared her the most—and came out of it a better version of herself.

I've met some pretty remarkable students during my nineteen years of teaching. Elaine is that rare student who defies the usual classifications—she's truly a "*unique snowflake of special unique specialness*" (one of her favorite lines from *Fight Club*). I know that whatever she does, it will be remarkable. And you'll want to be there, too, even for a small part of it—if for no other reason than to say that you knew her when.

INTERVIEWS WITH THE VAMPIRES

How to Take the Horror out of Interpersonal Communication

CHAPTER 10

Everybody's talkin' at me.
I don't hear a word they're saying,
Only the echoes of my mind.

— *Harry Nilsson, "Everybody's Talkin'"*

I ONCE BEGAN AN ADMISSIONS INTERVIEW by lobbing a softball question to a young man who was ranked in the top ten of his high school: "What have you been reading lately that wasn't assigned for school?"

The answer—as they tease on the internet—was SHOCKING!

"To tell you the truth," he said, "this is the first year I've read *any* of the books in my English class." He seemed genuinely proud that he had always made an A without doing the reading.

This student attended a well-known suburban feeder school and had all the requisite credentials, but his glib admission was galling.

Taking the bait, I asked how he managed to make such good grades without reading the books. He said that if he just listens to his teachers, then they will say pretty much what they want to hear. All he had to do was regurgitate what was said in class, randomly flip through the book for quotes, and that was it.

I mentioned that college was not going to be like high school—he would need to actually read the books. I sagely informed him that when professors assigned readings each week, they expected papers in which students engaged with the text.

I noted the disconnect between his grades and his academic engagement, and I summarized my frustration in my write-up: *this was a student who was not taking advantage of his educational opportunities.*

The student was ultimately denied.

Can I Get a Volunteer?

As we have pointed out, college interviews conducted by admissions officers carry more weight than those conducted by alumni volunteers. In fact, the tradition of using a volunteer army of interviewers has been backfiring on colleges over the past decade.

Most colleges cannot possibly have an admissions officer interview every applicant, so they rely on an alumni network to do some of the work. It used to be a win-win situation: colleges got the interviews done and alumni remained connected to their schools and served as community ambassadors.

The perception persists that the Ultras are exclusive enclaves that strive to keep undesirables out. And for decades in the early 20th century, the interview was a not-so-secret way for the schools to see in person what they could not ask on the application (race, wealth, and physical attractiveness, among other factors).

PRO TIP: If a college does not offer interviews with admissions officers, do not insist on having one. The admissions officer will most likely meet with you and ask if you have any questions while you stare back and wait to be questioned. This awkward situation is almost always mom or dad's idea: "Let them put a name with a face because you are so much more than what you appear on paper!"

But with admissions rates shrinking, the alumni are mounting a mutiny because the top schools are not accepting the students that the alumni are enthusiastically endorsing. Of course, every alumni interviewer wants some say as to which students make up the five percent of accepted students, but interviewers sometimes go years without having a student admitted, so it is unsurprising that they lose interest.

There are only so many interviews a person will do (for free) without any of their recommended students getting accepted. First they quit volunteering to interview, and then they quit donating money.

What was once a lovely symbiotic relationship has been damaged by ever-plummeting acceptance rates.

So what does all this mean for students applying to college today?

GET REAL: It's a familiar refrain: the more exclusive the school, the more material they are likely to collect on applicants. When it comes to the overall importance of interviews, few schools require them, and even fewer consider them an important part of the decision-making process. In 2006, only 10 percent of schools considered them important, dropping to just four percent in 2014.

As an applicant, your job is to make sure that your interview does not turn into a disaster like the namesake 2014 movie with James Franco and Seth Rogen that wound up at the center of an international crisis between Sony Pictures and North Korea.

Why So Serious?

The college interview is one of the most terrifying elements of the college process for many students, especially introverts or those with limited English-speaking skills.

The interview also takes place away from parents (which is a plus for many students) and on unfamiliar turf, whether it's at the college, office of an alumni interviewer, or somewhere else like a library, restaurant, or coffee house.

Unlike the college essay, which students can perfect over weeks or months, the interview typically lasts 20 to 40 minutes, and there is no do-over. But like an essay, the best interviewees put in plenty of advance work.

A lot of preparation goes into that interview, so here's some things you should do, and why.

BEFORE THE INTERVIEW

Regardless of who will be conducting your interview, you should immerse yourself in facts about the college and be prepared to make small talk about what's happening on campus.

Do you know how the football team is doing? Even if you have not cultivated an interest in team sports, you should at least present yourself as a person who has some school spirit. And if you can mention the result of a recent rivalry game, you might be able to bridge the generation gap between a rabid alumna and yourself.

In 2014, one of my newspaper editors was interviewing at Duke, and when she was asked about her proudest moment in high school, she told them about the time that our little newspaper website got 17,000 visits in one day, all because we had wall-to-wall coverage, including live streaming, of the announcement by blue chip basketball star Justise Winslow regarding where he would attend college.

When Winslow proclaimed he was going to Duke, a gymnasium full of students went bonkers, and the newspaper staff went into overdrive tweeting, taking photos, posting articles, and editing video. For our fledgling online platform, which my editor had launched her sophomore year, this felt like big-time journalism.

Turns out, the Duke interviewer was one of those 17,000 people glued to their computer screen to find out if the Blue Devils were going to land another top recruit. My editor was admitted, and she was on campus the next year when Justise helped Duke win the 2015 National Championship.

What's Happening?

Do some online research to see what's big news around campus, but you should also read the past few issues of the college newspaper. If you are ever on campus, definitely pick one up, paying special attention to the front page and the op-ed section. There are also a multitude of online forums where you can get some of the nitty-gritty about a university.

Maybe you are hesitant to bring up negative stories like cheating scandals, campus sexual assaults, or state budget cuts, but you should be aware of them. You have every right to talk to your interviewer about these topics since you may end up being associated with the school.

Besides the massive admissions scandal of 2019, over the past decade, other major scandals have rocked some of the most well-known schools in the country:

155

In 2012, roughly 125 Harvard students were suspected of cheating on a final exam, and after an investigation, 70 students were forced to withdraw.

In 2014, it was reported that many athletes at the University of North Carolina had been taking "paper classes" in order to maintain academic eligibility. UNC has since paid public relations firms over $500,000 to help repair the damage.

High profile sexual assault cases at Stanford, Columbia, Virginia, Baylor, Duke, and Dartmouth have been all over the news. While some of these stories are ongoing, some have been recanted (*Rolling Stone* had to backtrack on their UVA story) and some students have been exonerated (Duke lacrosse players).

The 2011 revelations about Penn State coach Jerry Sandusky's sexual misconduct with young boys not only stained the reputation of the school but forever tarnished the legacy of long-time head coach Joe Paterno, who was thought of as a quasi-religious icon in Pennsylvania. Sexual assault scandals have also embroiled Michigan State, Ohio State, and Georgia Tech, among others, in recent years.

Whether or not you know or care about these issues, if you are applying to a school where serious news is happening, you should at least be informed.

PRO TIP: Try not to schedule too many interviews close together. An admissions officer at a liberal arts college in New England tells a story about a student who began her interview by admitting that she forgot where she was—her mom had scheduled such a whirlwind college tour that the student simply could not remember where she was interviewing. The admissions officer felt sorry for her and offered up a cup of tea. No, it did not doom her admissibility, but it does make for an amusing cautionary tale.

Pleased to Meet Me

Sometimes you will know in advance the name of the person conducting the interview, so it stands to reason that you could do a little digging. You do not need to prepare a full CIA dossier on your interviewer, but find out enough to discuss their job or other interesting factoids you stumble across during the conversation. It's a plus if they work in a field you find interesting. Make sure you know how to pronounce their name and how to address them (Mrs./ Ms./Dr.?).

If you are serious about interviewing, you should practice with someone who has actually done interviews before. It could be a school counselor, teacher, or family friend (maybe someone with experience working in human resources).

The more often you do anything, the more comfortable you will be and the better you will perform. There are those who wing it and those who prepare, but if you are not a particularly adept conversationalist, a little prep time never hurt.

Come and Join Our Party Dressed to Kill

Back in the 1990s, I was an alumni interviewer. Before an interview, I always spoke to the kids and warned them that I was not going to be dressed up, so they shouldn't be either. Comfortable or dressy casual was fine. You know, a shirt with a collar and shoes with no logos.

It always saddened me when a kid arrived in a suit and tie, either because he did not remember my instructions or the parents refused to believe him.

PRO TIP: Do not show up for your Vanderbilt interview wearing a Duke shirt or University of Tennessee orange.

If You Cannot Be There On Time, Get There Early

Do not be late. Do not be late. Do not be late. Or as a Forbes once stated: "5 Minutes Early is On Time; On Time is Late; Late is Unacceptable."

DURING THE INTERVIEW

If you have not read Dale Carnegie's self-help classic *How to Win Friends and Influence People* (originally published in 1936), you should. It is certainly better than anything Dr. Phil has written. If you have the time after you finish *this* book, then go check out Carnegie's.

Carnegie posited that in order for people to like you, you just have to get them talking about themselves. Here are his six rules:

(1) Become genuinely interested in other people.

(2) Smile.

(3) Remember that a person's name is, to that person, the sweetest and most important sound in any language.

(4) Be a good listener. Encourage others to talk about themselves.

(5) Talk in terms of the other person's interest.

(6) Make the other person feel important—and do it sincerely.

In Chuck Palahniuk's *Fight Club*, the insomniac narrator observes that when people think you are close to death "they really, really listen to you, instead of just waiting for their turn to speak." Neither you nor your interviewer needs to be terminal, but taking a genuine, active interest in people goes a long way.

Smiling and other nonverbal cues are invaluable. And if you believe the pseudo-science, you should sit on the right of the person you want to impress.

A few other suggestions:

- DO NOT check your cellphone during the interview. Turn it OFF. Not even on vibrate.
- DO NOT chew gum.
- DO give a firm handshake—but DO NOT try to crush anyone's fingers.
- DO NOT drink soda before the interview (the last thing you need is to be gassy).
- DO NOT drink too much of any liquid. You will not want to excuse yourself during the interview.
- DO maintain eye contact.
- DO NOT curse or use slang (In the film *50/50*, Seth Rogen reports, "My date did not go well, unfortunately. Due to a lack of chemistry and, I think, an overuse of profanity on my part.")
- DO NOT twirl if you sit in a swivel chair, and do not bounce your legs absentmindedly. Maintain good posture.
- DO NOT use too many "like" and "you know" interjections—they will undercut your perceived intelligence. Avoid beginning answers with "Uhm" as well. If you need time think of an answer, you can always start with "That's a great question," which buys you time and compliments your interviewer.

And do not be sycophantic by faking an interest in the interviewer. Just watch Danny Noonan try (and fail) to impress Judge Smails in *Caddyshack*:

DANNY
I planned to go to law school after I graduated, but it looks like my parents won't have enough money to put me through college.
JUDGE SMAILS
Well, the world needs ditch-diggers, too.

Sometimes you might be offered an interview for admission or a scholarship via Skype or some other form of video chat. The same rules of interviewing apply, but take additional care to ensure that you are somewhere quiet, with good lighting, and that there is nothing inappropriate in the background. It is a good idea to perform a sound and video check prior to your online interview. Nothing kills the mood faster than "I can't hear you!"

"I GET THE FEELING WE'RE PRESSED FOR TIME."

The Question to Everyone's Answer Is Usually Asked from Within

The interview playbook is not that complicated. Interviewers work from a basic script. They get some general info at the outset and then try to cover the main questions provided by the university. While some alumni might go rogue, you should count on questions that are similar in content to a lot of your college essays and supplements.

Some interviewers prefer specific questions like "What do you plan to study?" Others prefer the open-ended prompts like "Tell us about yourself." Be prepared for both.

You should also expect questions like these:

- Why do you want to attend College X? (Sometimes it's painfully obvious that a student does not really want to attend the school and will sabotage the interview by flat-out admitting that they are only applying because their parents made them).
- How did you challenge yourself in high school?
- What are your educational and/or career goals?

- What do you like to do in your free time?
- What is your biggest flaw? (Yes, you can give one of those answers that sounds like a flaw but is really a positive—*I try to do too much and tend to overschedule myself with work, sports, and charitable endeavors.*) Think of a solid answer beforehand or you might find yourself spontaneously over-sharing.
- If you could do anything differently, what would it be?
- Have you read anything good lately? (Yes, they still ask this.)

At some point, your interviewer will probably ask if you have any questions. Do not pass on the opportunity, but do not ask silly questions that can be answered by looking on the school website.

Don't Ask Me Why

Every year I teach my journalism students how to conduct an interview, and one major point is about how to frame a question. Avoid asking WHY questions. Ask HOW questions instead.

If you ask someone, "Why did you become a doctor?" it sounds like they have to justify the decision, and thus the answer becomes defensive.

If you ask that same person "How did you become a doctor?" then you will get a story—and often a much better one than if you keep asking people WHY?

To get the interviewer talking, try using these conversation energizers:

- (If they are an alumni) "How did *you* make the decision to attend Tufts?" (Remember, do not ask WHY).
- "Besides interviewing, how do you stay/get involved in life at Stanford?"
- "What are three things students should do at Emory before they graduate?"
- "How has Notre Dame changed since you graduated/first started working here?"

This is a conversation, not a series of monologues. If you listen to Dale Carnegie, you will realize that the more you can get the other person talking, the better the interview will go.

At the conclusion of the interview, shake hands again, thank them by name, and be on your way.

AFTER THE INTERVIEW

Follow up with a thank-you note. An email is good. A personal, handwritten letter is better. This is non-negotiable.

And if you are accepted, send your interviewer another letter to thank them for helping make it possible. Who knows, if that person is in admissions, they may go to bat for you when it comes time to award scholarship money; if they are an alumna, they might help you get an internship or job someday.

GET REAL: Seniors are always dashing off to admissions interviews. During peak season, it is not uncommon to see one of my newspaper editors working on pages, then excuse herself to change out of her school uniform and into her interview clothes, drive to an interview, and come back an hour later like nothing happened. Such is the reality of applying to more than ten Ultras—you are going to have a lot of interviews.

Super-Selective Scholarships

Even if you are admitted to a school that does not require an interview, students vying for scholarships may need an interview. Some scholarships, like the elite Jefferson Scholars at the University of Virginia, have all 120 finalists come to campus for four days in the spring during which students participate in seminars, complete a writing assessment based on one of those classes, take a math/logic exam, and have a personal interview.

One of my editors, who was named a Jefferson Scholar finalist, described the process as an academic Hunger Games. Of the finalists, 34 students found out that they got the scholarship just 24 hours after Selection Weekend ended. Interestingly, my editor really wanted to be nominated for a Morehead Scholarship at the University of North Carolina, but another student was nominated by the school for that scholarship. Even though she didn't get a chance at her first-choice scholarship, my editor wound up with a nice $240,000 consolation prize.

During the Jefferson Scholars Selection Weekend in 2015, one enthusiastic young man decided to engage in the UVA practice of "Streaking the Lawn," a venerable tradition of dashing across the lawn *au naturale*. During his naked dash, he was spotted by one of the scholarship panelists. The next day, during his interview, the panelist asked him about his streaking experience. To his credit, the student owned up to it and, in the end, was named a Jefferson Scholar. Seems they appreciated his enthusiasm and candor.

This is not an endorsement of public exhibitionism, but if this student had been overly embarrassed or lied about the incident, then it might not have turned out so well.

The lesson: Sometimes interviews can expose more than expected.

Where Else Are You Applying?

If you are being interviewed by a college employee, you are unlikely to field inquiries about your other applications. Even most alumni interviewers have been told not to ask, but that does not mean someone will not try.

If you follow college sports, you know that there is an entire industry that reports on which colleges are likely to sign blue chip athletes, but everyday students might not like the idea of people asking where else they are applying. We already know students do not like telling other students, their relatives, or their teachers where they are applying, so why would they divulge this information to a stranger?

The NACAC Code of Ethics says that colleges should not be asking students where else they are applying (except in the case of early enrollment applicants who must enroll if admitted). But what to do if you get asked anyway? (Almost always, this will be from an alumnus who does not know any better than not to ask.) You could tell the interviewer "I am applying Early Decision to _____, so if I get in, that is where I plan to attend." Or you could say, "I have many options for pursuing my further education, but I choose not to discuss them with anyone outside my family. Try not to blurt out: "None of your business!"

The Final Frontier

William Shatner, Captain James T. Kirk himself, once said, "I sometimes find that in interviews you learn more about yourself than the person learned about you."

When it comes to college interviews, it is more important that you get interviewed than knock it out of the park. It's not a graded assignment; colleges want to make sure you are a reasonably intelligent and interesting person.

Just don't totally screw it up by admitting that you don't read anything.

THE MYTH OF THE TUBA PLAYER FROM WYOMING

CHAPTER 11

Living in your own Private Idaho,
Underground like a wild potato.

— *B-52's, "Private Idaho"*

ONE STORY I HAVE HEARD FOR YEARS, whether working in undergraduate admissions or college counseling, is this notion that admissions offices are searching for students with a talent in a given extracurricular activity. This desired activity can be a performing art or an uncommon sport. Often, the desired student is, remarkably, an accomplished tubist.

Ah, the legendary tuba player! Allegedly and apparently, this rarified applicant once had an incredible run with colleges across the country. There was not a single school that could resist the musical stylings of this brass-playing virtuoso. Adding to the irresistibility of this tubist was the fact that he was from Wyoming, Alaska, Idaho, or one of the Dakotas (I get them confused). Admissions committee after admissions committee just swooned after hearing his full-bodied sound, and like any good suburban legend in college admissions, the student was naturally admitted everywhere he applied.

The tuba player from Wyoming is the quintessential example of how a little bit of truth within the admissions process (which can arguably be esoteric and opaque to many) can become mythologized within the culture of the college search process. In fact, a cursory internet search of "tuba player college admissions" yields some interesting results.

Let me bust this proverbial bubble and put anxious students at ease.

Every college is trying to fulfill their institutional goals, which can include students who possess a given talent such as athletics and fine arts. So yes, the statement "colleges are looking for a tuba player" is possibly true, but that statement must be couched with the facts like *there are not many tuba players and colleges might only need a few of them.* Bands and orchestras might only have one tuba player (and musicians do not get a redshirt year like athletes). In other words, colleges are not admitting tubists by the dozen. It should also be noted that this myth always fails to mention anything about the famed tuba player's academic record or other qualifications.

The same holds true for students from the least populated states. I cannot tell you how many college information sessions I have attended in which someone makes a comment about how the college "needs someone from Montana." The reality? There are not that many high school students in these states, and even fewer who venture out of state, so the prospective applicant pool barely breaks double digits at some colleges.

There are six U.S. states with total populations under one million people (Montana actually has just a bit more than one million). So, to put it into perspective, there are more people in San Diego than all of Montana. Indianapolis has more residents than North Dakota. And Milwaukee has a greater population than Wyoming.

In many admissions offices, if one student from a sparsely populated state is admissible, they very well might be admitted. Why? Because it's cool to say you have students from all 50 states, even if the entire Montana student delegation to a university equals the number of people they send to the U.S. House of Representatives (that would be one).

While I have heard of left-handed South Dakotans that play the accordion, the reality is that those students are unicorns in Admissions Land.

What colleges want are genuine students who will create a community of learners, thinkers, and players. No music lessons or moving to Big Sky Country required.

Guess Who's Coming to College?

The overall rate of college enrollment is up across all racial groups since the 1980s, but it's a much different picture when the most selective schools are examined.

According to the Brookings Institute, African-American students make up just four percent of all students at the top 96 schools in the nation while 59 percent attend schools ranked in the bottom half. In comparison, 29 percent of Asian students attend the same top 96 schools.

Affirmative action policies are in place at a number of colleges to help level the playing field for underrepresented minorities, but these same rules tend to work against Asian students.

UPenn student columnist Benjamin Zou, who is Asian, wrote in the Daily Pennsylvanian about a conversation he had as a junior in high school with a white friend who claimed to love affirmative action. When Zou asked him why, the white student replied, "Because affirmative action benefits everyone, except Asians."

As noted earlier, the Asian population at the most selective colleges hovers around 20 percent. A controversial 2005 Princeton University study quantified how student SAT scores were assessed by colleges according to race, and the results seemed to verify a bias against Asian applicants.

According to the Princeton study, SAT scores (using a 1600-point scale) for white students were taken at face value while African-Americans received a "bonus" of 230 points and Hispanic students got 185 points. Meanwhile, Asian students were essentially penalized 50 points.

That same study also determined that recruited athletes gained 200 points and legacy applicants got a bonus of 160. The greatest underrepresented minority advantage was given to African-American and Hispanic students with SAT scores in the 1200-1300 range.

For many observers, the current de facto quota system imposed on Asian students is reminiscent of the tactics employed by Harvard and other Ivy League schools in the 1920s to limit the number of Jewish students.

As the Trump administration seeks to end Obama-era guidelines that encourage colleges to utilize race as a basis for college admission, it remains to be seen what impact it will have on the overall composition of incoming college classes.

GET REAL: Sometimes where you went to high school matters. In 2013, the Harvard Crimson noted that five percent of incoming Harvard freshmen came from just seven feeder schools. Meanwhile, 74 percent of admitted students came from high schools in which they were the only person admitted to Harvard. Even more amazing, the BBC reported in 2018 that over half the students that attended Oxford and Cambridge (from 2015 to 2017) came from *just eight schools.*

Extra Extracurriculars! Read All About It!

So the myth of the tuba player has been dispelled, but what isn't fantasy is that colleges do expect students to have engaged deeply in extracurricular activities.

The worst-kept secret in college admissions is that **colleges are not looking for well-rounded kids; they are looking for a well-rounded class.**

Take any sports team you like—you need a variety of skills to make a team successful. The New England Patriots would be terrible if they had 45 clones of Tom Brady. Sure they would be set at quarterback, but who is going to block or play defense? Baseball teams need sluggers and speedsters and fielders and pitchers (lefty and righty; starters and relief specialists). Mike Trout is an amazing outfielder, but he would be a liability if he were asked to play shortstop or pitch. And you can only imagine a basketball team that starts five point guards or had a bench made up exclusively of centers.

Colleges would ideally like to have students with a variety of interests, but do any actually help your chances?

Let's take a look at the Rice University profile for the 1,048 freshmen accepted for the Class of 2021. Of those freshmen, here's what they did outside the classroom:

Community Service (869)	Research (212)
Varsity athletics (486)	Student government (188)
Organization President (355)	Solo voice/choir (71)
Band/orchestra (246)	Student Council President (17)
Drama/debate (220)	Class President (16)

On the surface, volunteer work does not set one apart, but everyone is doing it. So consider doing your fair share, but going all-in with volunteer work will not guarantee much, especially if your application shows that you only participated in the class service project or logged the mandatory 100 service hours.

Student Council President or Senior Class President is a pretty good indicator of a quality applicant—and there can only be one each per school.

Participating in theater or debate is just about as common as playing in band or orchestra, and being in student government has roughly the same level of interest as those who engaged in research activities.

GET REAL: After looking at some school profiles, do not rush right out and push your kids to participate in certain activities. If your son loves working with the Robotics Club, do not make him join debate. If your daughter is passionate about lacrosse, do not force her to run for student council.

So if you are a varsity athlete who does community service, then you are less likely to stand out, and if you are the Student Council President and solo in choir, then you are more unique.

Some families might think it's a good idea to load up on as many extracurricular activities as possible, but many colleges limit the number of activities that can be mentioned on an application (MIT only allows four), so it's wiser to be judicious with one's time and participate in activities that are more meaningful and fulfilling.

To Tell the Half-Truth

Here is an ethical dilemma: Let's say you are a co-editor-in-chief of the yearbook or one of two Drama Club presidents, or one of the four football team captains. Should you mention how many others share the honor, or should you just say you are the Editor-in-Chief, President, or Captain?

The Solution: Always state that you share the honor or position. One of your rec letters might mention that you share responsibility, and if you do not come clean about it, you will look like you are trying to take more credit than you deserve.

The Sporting News

When athletes begin high school, they often play multiple sports. At small schools, it's not uncommon for even mediocre athletes to play three varsity sports. At large schools, coaches do not like to share athletes—unless they are blue chippers—and then they learn to share. Bo Jackson and Deion Sanders and Jameis Winston could all play NCAA football and baseball, but those are the rarest of exceptions.

The reality is that, according to the NCAA, a ridiculously small percentage of high school athletes will play in college. How small? For most sports, the odds of playing a Division I sport are worse than the overall acceptance rate at Harvard.

The best bet for boys is ice hockey, which has 4.8 percent of high school players going on to compete at the Division I level. The brutal truth is that many sports only have one percent (or fewer) students playing DI, including basketball, volleyball, and wrestling.

For girls, the numbers are similar. Ice hockey (8.8 percent) freezes the competition. No other sport has more than four percent making it to DI.

The somewhat encouraging news is that there are highly selective colleges that play Division III athletics, including a whole host of small elite schools. The percentage of athletes in DIII is roughly the same as in DI, but with a few exceptions. For boys there are almost three times more lacrosse players in DIII (7.1 percent) than DI (2.5) and more than twice as many in soccer (2.7 to 1.3). For girls there is a sizable increase in field hockey (5.7 to 3.0) and lacrosse (6.2 to 3.7).

This should not be breaking news—it is incredibly hard to play competitive sports, and it's even harder to balance athletics with academics. The hope for many kids is that sports can put student-athletes on a path to college admission, even if other aspects of the student's file are not as impressive.

Here is where the gamesmanship comes in. We all know kids who play fringe sports that are not available at most high schools: squash, crew, sailing, gymnastics, figure skating, fencing, et cetera. Do they have a leg up on the general population? By now you should know the answer—it depends.

If you are an amazing male gymnast—not Olympics level, but good—you have just 16 Division I programs to choose from, and three are service academies. So if you do not want to join the military after graduation, your options vary from Stanford and Cal to Michigan and Oklahoma (the 2016 and 2017 men's and women's champions).

Only the Ivy League, four ACC schools and roughly a dozen other universities field a co-ed DI fencing team, and a dozen more schools have DIII co-ed teams.

And for the intrepid few that play squash, there are 31 schools fielding teams for both men and women.

There are fewer than three dozen schools with DI women's team bowling.

If you are hoping to play football at Alabama, basketball at Duke, or baseball at Vanderbilt, the odds are not in your favor. But if you want to play Ivy League sports, your odds of getting in just went way up over the general population. Harvard fields 39 NCAA teams, while UCLA has only 22. Stanford has 36 varsity teams, yet Michigan has 25.

The big difference is that Ivy League schools do not offer athletic scholarships like the big state schools. Roughly 20 percent of an Ivy League freshman class is dedicated to recruited athletes, so as long as you are in contact with a coach, you may be all set.

Lies, Damned Lies & Statistics

It has been widely said that the lottery is a tax on those who are bad at math. If that is the case, then applying to the Ultras is kryptonite for those who are good at math. It is often shocking how many kids with perfect SAT scores do not comprehend that if a school has an acceptance rate of 10 percent, then there is a 90 percent chance that they will not get admitted.

Let's look at this another way: The odds of getting struck by lightning—twice—in your lifetime (and this assumes that you survive the first lightning strike) is 1 in 9 million. *But that will never happen to me.* When the Powerball jackpot reached a record $1.6 billion in January 2016, the odds of winning were 1 in 292 million. *Hey, someone's gotta win, why not me?*

It is baffling how many students do not seem to notice the single-digit acceptance rates at some of these schools. According to the numbers, it is much harder to get into these schools than it is to graduate from them. For the sake of comparison, the average college graduation rate is 50 percent in four years. Here are some random data points based on acceptance rates from the fall 2018 entering class and graduation rates from students who began in the fall of 2008:

	% Accepted	% Graduated
Stanford	4.3	75
Harvard	4.6	86
Yale	6.3	86
Columbia	5.5	86
Princeton	5.5	89

Judging by this small set of data, instead of applying to Stanford, should you apply to Princeton, which is ever-so-slightly "easier" to get into and thereby increase your chance of graduating on time by 14 percent?

PRO TIP: When looking at graduation rates, be sure to check the four-year rates. If you graduate in five or six years, you might be looking at an spending additional $120,000.

Keeping the Faith

To illustrate how statistics can be bandied about to show just about anything, consider the 2012 presidential campaign when Republican candidate Rick Santorum bemoaned that 62 percent of students who went to college would leave without their "faith conviction." It turned out that his numbers were a bit low (actually 64 percent for students attending a traditional four-year college); however, he failed to mention that *those who did not attend college lost their religion at a higher rate*—76 percent. Santorum also said President Obama was a "snob" for wanting as many kids as possible to attend college.

Whether you are contemplating religion or college admissions, they both require a leap of faith.

The Best Exotic Marigold College

There are roughly 3,000 four-year colleges in the United States, but if you ask your friends and family, there might as well just be 30. Julie Lythcott-Haines, a former Stanford dean of freshmen and author of *How to Raise an Adult*, wonders why high students think that being in the top five percent is considered excellent in high school but not when looking at colleges. Shouldn't all these high-achieving students find something to love in the Top 150 schools? Or the top 10 percent, roughly 300 schools?

Consider that in the United States, only five percent of high school graduates live on campus at a four-year college within one year of graduating from high school. Furthermore, of the 20 million American college students, only 10 percent live on campus. And from this small sliver of all college-bound students, an even smaller group is competing to get into the most elite and supremely impossible colleges and universities in the history of the known universe! **Just three percent of all high school students will attend a college that accepts fewer than 50 percent of its applicants.**

Lythcott-Haines has some simple rules for helping parents raise adults, especially during the college application process. One piece of advice she gives is for parents to "put independence in the way" of their kids. So, for example, if you are a parent reading this book and highlighting the most pertinent parts for your kid, you might not be presenting your child with enough opportunities to become the independent person they will need to be once they leave home (and you do want them to leave home eventually, right?). On the other hand, if you are a student who sought out this book and are reading it on your own—good job, kid. You are going to be just fine.

GET REAL: But what if you don't play the tuba? There are myriad factors that determine if you are admissible at highly selective colleges. If your heart is set on an Ultra, and you have strong grades in challenging courses along with a 1500 SAT or 34 ACT, then you have about a 20 percent chance of getting in.

Unsolved Mysteries

Much like the Loch Ness Monster and Bigfoot, the legend of the tuba player from Wyoming (or Montana) has taken on a life of its own and is unlikely to go away soon. But maybe you are a spelunker from Idaho, an apiarist from North Dakota or a graffiti artist from New Mexico. Whatever your skill or interest, do it because you enjoy it, not because it gives you a perceived advantage in college admissions.

THE MAN BEHIND THE CURTAIN PAYS A LOT OF ATTENTION

CHAPTER 12

Every breath you take
Every move you make
Every bond you break
Every step you take
I'll be watching you.

— The Police, *"Every Breath You Take"*

A S A FORMER ADMISSIONS OFFICER turned college counselor, I must admit (pun intended) that most students, families, and a healthy number of teachers, administrators—and even some college counselors—believe one unfounded truth: Admissions officers are stupid.

It did not matter whether I was on the college side or the high school side; I saw, and continue to see, this behavior. Everyone on the outside frets and worries, often with misplaced, unwarranted concern about the admissions office "not understanding" their student or their high school.

These anxieties are manifested differently. I have had families worry about whether or not Admissions was going to read a student's application in full and with appropriate attention to detail. I have also heard folks say (with zero evidence) that *they know there are cut-offs* for admission or "quotas" for accepting students from a given high school or specific geographic region.

These conspiracy theories are almost never true.

And yet...

It depends.

People associated with rigorous private or public high schools worry about whether or not the admissions office "knows how much stronger" their high school is than *other* schools in town. Never mind that their wealthy feeder school sends dozens of students to the Ultras every year.

POMPOUS MOM
If my child attended [that other school], she would practically be valedictorian!

DELUSIONAL DAD
If we lived in New Mexico instead of Manhattan, our kids would have an easier time getting into Harvard.

Ever wonder why, if these parents are so convinced of how much better their kids would fare if they attended another school or lived in another state, that they don't just send their kid to that school or move the entire family? And since that "other" school is usually a public school, they could save over $100,000 in tuition that they could then use for college.

Another common worry from parents (and often a dead giveaway that they have hired an independent college counselor or consultant) is if they call a meeting with the in-house college counselor and fret about whether the high school will properly communicate their child's "story" to the college admissions office.

High school administrators and the Board of Trustees alike will worry if "the colleges know how rigorous we are as a school" and will sometimes (foolishly) send a college counselor to the most selective colleges to explain all about their high school.

The quixotic notion is always the same: If they only knew how great we are as a school, then more of our students would be admitted!

In both scenarios, parents think the student is so great—and the administrators think the school is so great—so achieving admission should be all but guaranteed. The only possible reason that students are not getting into these schools is that someone else must have made a mistake!

This fallacy is strikingly naïve. The idea that college admissions offices, which spend about half their organizational efforts recruiting and trying to understand the vast array of high school communities, course offerings, grading scales, extracurricular options, pedagogical philosophies and the like, are somehow *not* attuned to the nuances of the students and their high schools makes the perceived aloofness (or incompetence) of the admissions office a most convenient scapegoat.

Assuming ignorance on the part of Admissions is a pretty arrogant worldview. *Our student/high school is so awesome that if you don't see how awesome they are, then clearly something is wrong with you!*

Is every admissions office fully adept at understanding each and every high school and student profile? Of course not, but the anxiety associated with perceived admissions officer ignorance is so common that the opinion of the general public might never be swayed.

Don't Keep a Low Profile

Almost all high schools will send a **school profile** that allows the admissions office to holistically understand that school's curriculum, grading scale, teaching philosophy, and college-going culture (among other factors). Admissions officers will use this document as a lens through which to view the student's record. Unless the high school has some truly unusual attribute, an experienced admissions officer will be able to quickly understand the high school from reading this document, but parents may still worry about how unclear it will appear. This is no different than an investment banker being able to evaluate a stock portfolio or a baseball fan determining the quality of a player by looking at statistics. It may take a layperson significantly longer to decipher the data, but it's all there.

What's amazing, yet not surprising, is that many high schools have weak, incomplete, inaccurate, or out-of-date school profiles. Sadly, it's not uncommon for some schools to not even have a profile, which may be required by out-of-state colleges.

Admissions offices spend a significant amount of time teaching their admissions staff how to read applications. In most offices, staff training is done annually, and even veteran admissions officers participate to both mentor the new officers and to refresh themselves.

Often the admissions process is viewed by the public as something mysterious and opaque (spoiler alert: it's neither), but these meetings are where admissions officers hone the art and science of evaluating applicants.

It has become more commonplace to hear about admissions and financial aid being housed jointly under the internal umbrella term **enrollment management**. Basically, it's a fancy name for the department in charge of deciding who gets in, who gets funding (need-based or merit), and how that funding is appropriated.

Geo Dudes

Many admissions officers are assigned admissions territories called **geomarkets**. These are divisions within states that look similar to congressional districts, but with significantly less gerrymandering. For example, Tennessee has four geomarkets: the Chattanooga area (TN-01), east Tennessee (TN-02), west Tennessee (TN-03), and middle Tennessee (TN-04).

Geomarkets will never offer any sort of "ah ha!" moments, nor will you ever find admissions officers telling students about them (because it's utterly irrelevant), but they do reveal information about the origin of most applications.

If a state is shared by different officers working within different parts of the state, then you can assume the college receives a lot of applications from that state and they need more officers to cover it. If you want to get a sense of which territories get special attention, just look at where the highest ranking admissions officers travel. It's not uncommon to see the dean of admissions work with New York City, which is full of academically rigorous high schools. As fascinating as all this is to an admissions nerd like me, do not worry too terribly much about what geomarket your high school is in since it's highly unlikely to play a major role in admission.

Colleges are increasingly using Big Data and algorithms to predict where they can find potential students who are most similar to their most satisfied recent college graduates. Colleges can then assign admissions officers to both new and existing geomarkets in order to find students who fit their profile. In a perfect world, colleges will spend less time and money to find students, they will receive more applications, they will accept a lower percentage of applicants, a higher percentage of those who are accepted will enroll, and a greater percentage of those freshmen will eventually graduate within 4 to 6 years and have a positive educational experience with a job or graduate school waiting for them upon graduation.

GET REAL: When high schools bring me in as a guest speaker for their school community as an "admissions insider," the audience is always warm, engaged, and grateful. However, when I present almost the exact same information in the exact same way during a local college information session, I am frequently met with skepticism and a palatable dose of unease. There is something about being billed as an insider that plays into the notion that college admissions is some sort of a trick.

Undue Alarm about Anything and Everything

It is no fun denying admission to great students, but it's a reality of the job. Families are constantly looking for ways to "wow" the admissions committee, "stand out" in the process, or "really impress" colleges. **The truth is that what achieves admission is often quite straightforward: rigorous curriculum, solid grades, test scores within the profile, commendable involvement in almost any extracurricular activity, and a desire to learn.**

So many doubts about what might ultimately result in admission are often misplaced or based on misinformation. That quest for the secret handshake is real for many families. Whether or not anyone actually discovers the Holy Grail (or the "black box" as some like to call it) misses the point. Students and especially parents have a need to feel actively involved in the process. Everyone wants to pretend they are Mulder and Scully from the *X-Files* searching for the answers: *They want to believe that the truth is out there.*

GET REAL: You want to do a good job and be accurate with your application; however, if you fret over every little detail, you are likely overreacting and overthinking. For example, if you are paralyzed with fear over whether to write an opening salutation as "Dear John Smith," or "Dear Mr. Smith," then you might need to switch to decaf. Admissions officers are not looking for one minor error in order to deny a student.

Unlike a high school test or essay, colleges do not return unsuccessful applications to students with a grade and comments so they can do better next time. This lack of feedback allows applicants and their families to conjure up all kinds of conspiracy theories regarding admissions decisions. Student stress and parental panic are often intensified by the fear that *something will keep them out.* In Joseph Heller's *Catch-22*, Captain Yossarian notes, "Just because you're paranoid doesn't mean they're not out to get you." But in college admissions, this paranoia is baseless and assumes that admissions officers are the epitome of cynicism. I have had so many students in a panic over things that are not big concerns at all. I feel for them because they are not sure what does and does not matter.

The Usual Suspects

There is a reason why highly selective colleges are highly selective: a lot of people apply because a lot of people want to attend. The reasons for applying are as sincere as they are unfounded. In every high school, there are certain colleges that *everybody* applies to because, just like in the Geico commercials, they're college applicants— that's what they do. This herd mentality creates the "usual suspect" colleges in a particular high school community. There are also students who apply to colleges that are not among the typical cadre of application destinations—and college counselors love these students. It's exciting to see seniors take a bold step forward into the unknown (at least within their high school community).

I once had a student who seemed pretty set on attending a usual suspect college. He had a reputation for being a bit of a follower (not in a bad way, he just wanted to fit in—who doesn't?). He applied Early Action to (and got deferred by) a bunch of the usual suspects. He was perpetually, and predictably, close-but-no-cigar. I encouraged him to look at a college on the opposite side of the country. He applied, somewhat begrudgingly, and was later admitted Regular Decision. To my proud surprise, he eventually enrolled after visiting campus and discovered that he really liked it. That's the sort of win-win situation that college counselors love about advising students.

There are, inevitably, the usual suspects that are coveted by many seniors within a school community, which creates tension and competition. Classmates size each other up. Community members wonder why a certain college seems to admit more students than another (Hint: It's because more qualified students applied from that high school). Moms tell other moms that they know each other's children are applying to the same college.

GET REAL: Do you honestly believe an Ultra or other highly selective college has an astronomically low admit rate just because Becky with the Good Hair from your physics class applied, too? No. **The overwhelming competition for admission comes from beyond your high school.**

One of my colleagues was once asked by a student to discuss one of the usual suspects—a school where we had roughly 20 applicants annually. She informed him: "I know a lot of people want to go there, but I *really* want to go there." She then asked if he would call up the admissions office and tell them that. The counselor ended the request by simply asking: If you love the school so much, why didn't you apply Early Decision?

Then there was the mother who, unbeknownst to her son, asked me to tell a college that her son was very interested while most of his friends were applying there just as a safety school. I took a hard pass on that request.

GET REAL: Your reach school may be someone's target. Your target school may be someone else's reach. And either one could be someone's safety. Acknowledge and respect other people's choices.

Formalized demonstrated interest or Early Decision policies aside, **"really wanting to go" is not an institutional metric used in admissions.** There is zero chance that an Ultra is going to be impressed that you, like Liz Lemon on *30 Rock*, "want to go to there."

Where Those Application Fees Really Go

The admissions process is full of necessary evils, including deadlines for submitting applications and the tracking of the credentials that make up an applicant's file. For most colleges, the student submits the application and requests that testing agencies send standardized test scores to the colleges. Meanwhile, the high school sends the transcript and letters of recommendation.

Collating this much paperwork for thousands of applicants is a gargantuan task. Underneath the bright and shiny admissions office is a data processing department staffed by a few dozen hard-working professionals. All this department does is sort and track data. They are the unsung heroes of the admissions process. If you've ever wondered where all those application fees go, they are helping finance this vital operation.

Often college undergrads will assist with file sorting and the like. While these student workers are some of the best and brightest, they sometimes struggle with alphabetization and filing.

Are You an Appli-Can or an Appli-Can't?

Considering all the information submitted to colleges via email, snail mail, FedEx, carrier pigeon, and dirigible, inevitably some of it will get misfiled or lost.

If your last name is common (e.g., not *Accrocco*, but more like *Thompson*), you will likely suffer more misplaced credentials than your more unusually named peers. Just be prepared.

With precious few exceptions, this is not a cause for alarm.

GET REAL: This is not a cause for alarm! Quite often colleges will send out notifications to students that some piece of their application is missing, even when the credentials are in-hand and being processed. Do not blame disappointing admissions results on a misplaced credential. And above all, do not, do not, (please!) DO NOT blame your college counselor! That person might be the only one who can help you rectify the situation with the college—but not if you bite your counselor's head off.

"WAITER, THERE'S CRUSHING ACADEMIC EXPECTATION IN MY SOUP"

Chances are good you will not receive any "we're missing something" emails from a college. If you are the first-born child and your family is overly anxious to begin with, and it's your first-choice college, then you can safely assume that, because the admissions gods are sadistic pranksters, you will get many of these notifications—much to your college counselor's chagrin.

If and when you receive an email from a college informing you that something is missing, here's the procedure:

(1) Calm yourself down.
(2) Calm down Parent No. 1.
(3) Calm down Parent No. 2.
(4) Reassure your younger sibling that it will not happen to them.

(5) Find the family pet that has retreated from the panic to an undisclosed location.

(6) Politely and appropriately contact your counselor.

(7) Trust that it's going to be alright—a resubmission is fine.

PRO TIP: If you need reassurance that all is well after the resubmission of a credential, have your counselor email the college and ask, "Does this complete his/her file?" Counselors will do this to help a student when steps 1-7 above are replaced by utter panic.

Colleges are trying to complete their applications. It is a not a black mark against you if something gets lost. They will contact you to complete the application. They will not insinuate that you are not getting in or that they are mad at you. Chill out. They are just trying to help you complete the application.

WHAT TO EXPECT WHEN YOU'RE EXPECTING

CHAPTER 13

Wouldn't it be nice if we were older?
Then we wouldn't have to wait so long.

— *The Beach Boys, "Wouldn't It Be Nice"*

I N QUENTIN TARANTINO'S influential 1994 film *Pulp Fiction*, hit man Vincent Vega shares some theories with his boss's wife, Mia Wallace, about why Mia's husband Marcellus defenestrated a Samoan hit man out a four-story window, leaving him with a bit of a speech impediment. Vincent and his colleagues have some salacious theories, but Mia says that no one really knows why her husband acted that way. She rightly concludes, "When you little scamps get together, you're worse than a sewing circle."

Those sewing circles of yore have nothing on today's parents who overshare and whip themselves into a frenzy brought on by misinformation, secondhand news, and anecdotal evidence of dubious origin. As a college counselor, I know I am in trouble when a parent tells me, "I was just at lunch with some friends and I heard..."

Beware the Ladies Who Lunch (or the Dudes Who Golf or Whatever It Is When a Bunch of Guys Get Together). No one wants to be the person who refuses to talk about their kids and where they might go to college (or where the parents really want them to go), but there are also a lot of parents out there who overshare, and if you share with them, they will pass along your news to other friends and acquaintances. And like any good game of Telephone, by the time the news gets around, the original message will probably get lost in translation.

The Anti-Social Network

While the majority of students have moved to Snapchat and Instagram for their social media needs, their parents are firmly entrenched on Facebook. A growing field of social media research indicates that using Facebook makes its users feel more lonely, alienated, and envious than those who eschew the ubiquitous online platform.

Most adults carefully cultivate what they put on social media, preferring only to share good news, which can create an aura of perfection that does not actually exist. This façade of perfection is especially problematic when parents read all about the amazing college news regarding the children of their Facebook friends.

Liam got into Yale!
So proud of our Jasmine for getting a full-ride to Barnard!!
Aiden will be playing squash next year at Haverford!!!

Want to make people jealous? Post about how your child got into Princeton. Restrictive Early Action.

Want to make parents who have children applying Regular Decision to the Ultras certifiably insane? Try posting about how your child—the one who got into Princeton via Restrictive Early Action—is now going to go ahead and apply to all the other Ivies. You know, "just to see how she does."

"I REMEMBER BAGGING COLUMBIA ON A PARTICULARLY FOGGY NIGHT CLOSE TO THE EARLY DECISION DEADLINE..."

Such bald-faced trophy hunting does not go over well with most parents (or colleges for that matter) and often results in lengthy conversations behind your back about how your kid is going to "take the spot" of other highly qualified students from the same school or hometown.

Trolling for More Information

There is a point at which every parent starts doing a little independent internet research. You know, to find out the real scoop about how to get into college. Eventually they will find themselves on College Confidential.

I've been there. I know.

What began in 2001 as a free website designed to educate people as to how colleges select applicants and determine financial aid, College Confidential has, according to one of its founders, turned into "a forum for handicapping a student's odds of being admitted to the nation's most-selective colleges."

That founder, David Hawsey, left the website years ago. He says the site has become far too negative. The trolls have taken over. *My school is better than yours. You'll never get in there. Yadda Yadda Yadda.*

Especially problematic on College Confidential and other online forums is the overwhelming "Ivy lust," as Hawsey calls it. And even within the Ultras, there is a strictly delineated hierarchy. The acronym HYP (Harvard-Yale-Princeton) creates an upper stratification among the Ivies. Others broaden their horizons by mentioning HYPS (Stanford added) or HYPSM (for MIT).

Since leaving College Confidential, Hawsey has worked in the office of enrollment management for several colleges. Of his online creation, he once said, "I feel like I failed to carry out my original mission to its conclusion. The interest in prestige overran the intent."

The Paradox of Choice, Part II

In Jimmy Buffett's song "Don Chu Know," he observes, "Indecision may or may not be my problem." Sometimes the most stressful part of the college process is not in achieving admission but deciding where exactly to go after getting accepted by more than one school. After all, even if you apply to 20 schools and *only* get into two—that's still twice as many schools as you can attend next year!

If you are curious what other students have done when faced with a similar dilemma, you can check out Parchment.com, which offers a side-by-side college comparison tool. A few fun results:

Princeton (34%)	Yale (66%)
Smith (24%)	Wellesley (76%)
U.S. Military Academy (48%)	U.S. Naval Academy (52%)
USC (39%)	UCLA (61%)
UChicago (72%)	Northwestern (28%)
Amherst (31%)	Williams (69%)
Columbia (53%)	UPenn (47%)

The Waiting Is the Hardest Part

If you got into your Early Decision school and the financial aid is acceptable, then you can skip this part—you're already in.

If you apply Regular Decision, then you must resign yourself to months in limbo, but that does not mean you cannot improve your chances.

PRO TIP: If you accomplish something truly noteworthy after submitting your application, you can always contact colleges with an update—just email your admissions officer.

For the most part, there is not much to do from January to the end of March. There may be some interviews (as discussed in Chapter 10), and you should be on the lookout for scholarship opportunities, but in the meantime, go to class, learn for the sake of learning, enjoy spending the final few months with your classmates, and try not to let Senioritis derail all your hard work.

SUBURBAN LEGEND: Getting Uninvited

Can colleges rescind acceptances if you make bad grades in your final semester?

Yes. Yes they can.

Although it happens in extremely rare circumstances (*see UC Irvine, Chapter 5*), this is not generally a cause for alarm. Do not freak out if you are a straight-A student and you make a C in one class.

And just because you were accepted Early Decision does not mean your future is assured. All colleges include language in their notifications that says all offers of acceptance are contingent upon the successful completion of high school. If colleges receive a mid-year report riddled with C's and D's, you probably will not get into the best schools, and if you were accepted early, you might get a phone call from the college to ask just what the heck is going on.

A single bad grade might not cause a college to rescind an acceptance, but as ten would-be Harvard students found out in 2017, you can—and will—have your acceptance revoked if you create a Facebook group called "Harvard memes for horny bourgeois teens" that shares memes and other images that make light of child abuse and specific ethnic and racial groups. Harvard warns students that the school may withdraw an offer "if an admitted student engages in behavior that brings into question his or her honesty, maturity, or moral character." Social media is the easiest way for colleges to become aware of unsavory behavior, so be careful what you post.

The Long Goodbye

As a teacher, it is fascinating to work with second-semester seniors. Some are truly going down that Senior Slide—they have checked out mentally and are going through the motions academically. They will do the bare minimum to finish, and sometimes not even that.

Yet other students, unshackled by the pressure to do well in the name of college admissions, are a revelation: they loosen up, they engage in class, and they turn in some of their best work ever. Of course, this makes perfect sense. Seniors are preparing for college, and while there are quite a few students letting their skills rust, there are many students honing their abilities in advance of university life. Students may think that just getting into a coveted university is the ultimate reward, but they will discover, sooner or later, that college is rife with competition for grades, admission to graduate programs, and job offers.

Spring is when Senioritis becomes a full-blown pandemic in which otherwise responsible students begin to act in predictably unpredictable ways.

PRO TIP: Do not ask your counselor how low your grades can drop before schools change their mind on early admission. We are not going to give you permission to slack off.

My colleagues and I refer to the final semester, more specifically those weeks after Spring Break, as The Long Goodbye. It sometimes feels like every day is another Final This or Last That for the seniors. Frankly, it's exhausting. Until those final college notifications are announced, March is a complete washout.

April Fools

The irony is not lost on anyone: Colleges send out the majority of their notifications by April 1.

Perhaps attempting to avoid the inevitable April Fools jokes, many colleges have moved up their announcement cycle to the last week in March. The Ultras tend to stagger the news, so a few schools will send out emails or post the news on the student portal each day. MIT gets an early jump by announcing their results on Pi Day, March 14.

Schools rarely mail out the "fat envelopes" any longer (Georgetown has been a notable exception). In the name of fairness and sanity, colleges want everyone to know at the same time, so they cannot rely on the Postal Service to deliver the news the way that the Pony Express did for their parents.

In the quest to achieve simultaneous electronic admission communication, sometimes things can go terribly, horribly wrong:

2018: In March, the University of Michigan's College of Literature, Science and the Arts sent an email to all prospective transfer students congratulating them on their acceptance. Students were soon informed that the emails had been sent in error.

2017: In February, Columbia University's School of Public Health sent an email that said they were "delighted to welcome" 276 students. Less than two hours later, Columbia sent a follow-up email alerting each applicant that the acceptance notice was premature.

2016: In December, Tulane University sent out 130 emails that began, "I am pleased to welcome you to Tulane!" Unfortunately, these Early Decision students had not yet been admitted. A few hours later, Tulane sent a retraction email notifying the students that it had all been a computer coding error. "We've created an anxiety so deep for this group that there really aren't words to describe it," wrote Tulane admissions director Jeff Schiffman in a blog post. "I'll own up to it right now."

In April, SUNY at Buffalo mistakenly sent more than 5,000 acceptance letters due to an incorrect email list.

2015: Carnegie Mellon accidentally sent 800 acceptance emails to students applying to a graduate program in (wait for it) *Computer Science*. The fact that a computer error was to blame for dashing the hopes of computer science students applying to a school that prides itself on its technology expertise was doubly embarrassing.

2014: In December, Johns Hopkins sent acceptance letters to 300 students who had already been denied. Hours later the school confirmed the original notification—they didn't get in.

In March, Goucher College sent acceptance emails to 60 students who had been denied.

In February, MIT sent out an email that read, "You are on this list because you are admitted to MIT!" The problem was that the email was sent to hundreds of students who had already been admitted and hundreds more who were just applicants.

2013: In December, before any decision had been made regarding acceptance, 2,500 Fordham applicants received a financial aid letter congratulating them on their acceptance. Students were notified by the university about the error hours later. The following day students could log in to see if they were actually admitted or not.

2012: In January, Vassar accidentally sent "test letters" via email to 122 applicants: 46 of those students were actually accepted, 76 were denied.

In April, UCLA erroneously sent acceptance notices to almost 900 applicants.

2011: The University of Delaware website erroneously showed 61 applicants they had been accepted when they had actually been waitlisted or denied.

2010: George Washington University sent out approximately 200 early acceptance notifications, which it apologized for just hours later.

2009: The largest "oops" moment in college admissions history occurred when the University of California, San Diego, sent out acceptance emails to all 46,000 applicants. Only 18,000 were actually admitted, meaning 28,000 applicants got their hopes up before learning the truth hours later.

On April 1, NYU's graduate school of public policy sent 500 notices to students who were actually denied admission.

2007: In January, the University of North Carolina erroneously sent out roughly 2,700 emails with the wrong subject line, which congratulated students of their acceptance even though admissions decisions had not yet been made.

2006: In an email training session gone awry, the director of admissions for the University of California, Berkeley, law school sent congratulatory emails to all 7,000 applicants. Fewer than 850 were eventually admitted.

2004: After first accidentally allowing personal data from roughly 2,000 applicants (including SAT scores and Social Security numbers) to be viewable by other applicants, the University of California, Davis, accidentally informed all of its 6,500 accepted students that they had received a $7,500 scholarship (it was only intended for 850 recipients).

2003: Cornell sent admissions emails in February to 550 students who had already been rejected in December.

Understandably, students who find out that they are accepted will immediately get on social media to share the good news, but when the rug is pulled out from under them, the results can be devastating.

PRO TIP: Do not jump the gun. Wait a day (or week) before publicizing any personal news about college admissions.

Sticker Shock

It's one thing for colleges to accidentally inform applicants that they got in—only to rescind the offer hours later—but these situations are admittedly rare. What's worse (and far more common) is when students get accepted by a dream school only to find out from their parents that they cannot afford to attend.

Parents, you need to tell your child up front whether or not you are willing and able to send them to college—and that means *all* the colleges. Every year I deal with students who are understandably upset that their parents want them to attend the most affordable college option, not their top choice or best fit. **Families need to have the tough conversation before students apply.** Do not put off the unpleasant discussion and hope that your child will not get into the most expensive school. Your student will be justifiably angry if he or she gets in and *then* you break the bad news.

Every college website offers a Net Price Calculator to help families determine their expected family contribution. If the result is that you are expected to pay $70,000 a year, it's unlikely your student will receive any need-based aid.

In order to qualify for need-based aid, families must complete the Free Application for Federal Student Aid (FAFSA). An additional 300 colleges require families to complete both the FAFSA and the College Scholarship Service Profile as well.

While on a college visit with Child No. 1, I heard a parent ask the director of financial aid how long it would take to fill out the FAFSA online. The director said it would only take about 30 minutes.

Much hearty laughter erupted from the audience.

That's because the FAFSA is a beast. And if you are not a Certified Public Accountant, the task can be daunting. But if you want to be considered for need-based financial aid or have the opportunity to land a work-study job, then you should fill it out. Consider what might happen if an unforeseen death, divorce, or job downsizing happens to a family after the applications are submitted. If the FAFSA and CSS are complete, they can be quickly updated to reflect the change in circumstances.

Beginning in 2017-2018, parents could use their prior-prior year's tax returns to complete the FAFSA. Allowing parents to use the prior-prior year's returns meant that parents could file in October instead of January. For colleges, receiving the FAFSA earlier in the application process aligns the admissions and financial aid schedule, allowing them to make financial awards earlier, which in turn gives families more time to consider their options.

Of all the recent changes in financial aid, college counselors are quite happy about the prior-prior decision, and you should be, too.

Scholars Get Scholarships

If you've ever watched the Miss America Pageant, you might be aware that they tout themselves as the "world's largest provider of scholarships for women" and claim to provide almost $45 million in scholarships to its competitors.

In 2014, comedian John Oliver pointed out in a scathing report on *Last Week Tonight* that those numbers are highly deceiving. Miss America says that it provides all these scholarships, but what they *actually* do is *make these scholarships available*. And since contestants cannot accept more than one scholarship offer, the actual amount of money provided to these women is far less than advertised.

Like $44.5 million less.

That's right, according to Oliver, the Miss America Foundation awarded less than $500,000 in scholarships to women in 2012. In comparison, the Society of Women Engineers disbursed more than 230 new and renewed scholarships (valued at $715,000) in 2017—and there was no swimsuit competition.

Most scholarships, however, are used to recognize and attract talented students to an institution. As one higher education professor once said, "It's a bribe." Scholarships are a means to help build a class that meets the institutional goals, and as the competition for admission increases, the competition for scholarships does too. Many of the Ultras do not even offer merit scholarships since they will have little trouble assembling their freshman class every year, thank you very much.

The Ladder Rule stipulates that in college admissions, **a student always longs to be one rung higher on the admissions ladder than they currently are**:

If they are denied, they ask, "Can you please put me on the waitlist?"

Waitlisted: "Can't you please admit me?"

Admitted: "What, no scholarship?"

Admitted with a scholarship: "Couldn't I have more money?"

Admitted with full-ride scholarship: "No thanks. I'm going to an Ultra."

I Want You to Want Me, I Need You to Need Me

As noted in Chapter 5, some colleges give generously to National Merit Finalists, but you do not have to be recognized for amazing PSAT scores to get significant merit aid.

In-state public schools typically provide lower tuition costs but award less financial aid while private schools are more expensive yet have more merit aid at their disposal.

In 2014-2015, the five public schools that spent the most money on merit aid were the University of Alabama ($101 million), Ohio State University ($62 million), Indiana

University ($56 million), University of Michigan ($50 million), and Temple University ($48 million).

On the other end of the spectrum, the public schools that gave the smallest percentage of their financial aid budget to non-needy students were the University of Tennessee (0 percent), University of Texas at Austin (4 percent), University of California at Berkeley (6 percent), University of Virginia (6 percent), and University of North Carolina at Chapel Hill (7 percent).

When Bob Woodward and Carl Bernstein were chasing the Watergate story, their deep cover source told them to "follow the money." When it comes to doling out financial aid, **schools in need of revenue tend to use their money to chase wealthy students who can pay full price while colleges in need of prestige pursue students with high test scores.**

In a perfect world, colleges hope to increase both prestige and revenue from their applicant pool. From a student's perspective, they can make a better case for admission if they have something that the university needs. And sometimes the ability to pay trumps their academic credentials.

Undermatching and Overshooting

Undermatching is when a student accepts admission to a college, usually with a hefty scholarship, which is nonetheless below their perceived level of where they could have gone. While this term has some unfortunate and arguably unfair baggage, it illustrates the unofficial caste system that exists in America. The perception is that it's fine to aspire to a college above your station (based on GPA, board scores, or family income), but if you try applying below your station, then there must be something wrong with you.

Some enrollment managers acknowledge this reality. Consequently, part of their enrollment strategy might be that most any student who is admitted—and exceeds institutional goals—will receive a merit scholarship as a way of wooing them.

A variety of factors can lead a student to undermatch. On the one hand, there are high-achieving, underserved minority students who either do not bother applying to the Ultras or turn them down due to financial considerations (going to Harvard is expensive even with free or reduced tuition) or the familial pressure to stay close to home, just to name a few.

On the other hand, some students may have had their fill of the pressure-packed crucible of high school and would like a more laid-back college experience—especially if the school is willing to dole out some of that sweet, sweet merit aid to seal the deal. One student recently confided that after four years of high stress at an elite high school, they had no intention of applying to any Ivy League schools. His sound logic was that he went to a challenging top-flight private high school so he wouldn't feel inadequate in college. Why would he want all that anxiety for four more years?

What If You Don't Get In?

If you have done your research, listened to the admissions officers, heeded the advice of your college counselor, and read this book, then not getting in anywhere is a highly unlikely scenario. There is a reason all this information is available: to help you make sound decisions.

Every year there is some benighted senior who works out the probability of getting into college like this: *Let's see...UPenn has a 10-percent accept rate...and Dartmouth accepts 11 percent. So, as long as I apply to 10 schools that have about a 10-percent accept rate, I have a 100 percent chance of getting into one of them!*

If you do find yourself in a predicament like Richard III ("A college, a college! My kingdom for a college!"), do not panic. Well, okay, you are allowed to have a brief, controlled panic attack, but then get yourself together—there is always hope!

GET REAL: Even if you do not get into college by April 1, that does not mean anything officially about your future. Yes, it is disappointing and can be scary, but you still have options.

Every year after Decision Day, plenty of great colleges still have space and will accept applications (see Chapter 3 for a few of the roughly 300 schools that typically have room for freshmen in August!). Many distraught students in dire straits have ended up studying at these institutions and gone on to live a happy, successful lives. A current list of colleges seeking students is easily accessed by your college counselor.

You could also take a gap year, which can be great for students who want to pursue an internship, paying job, volunteer work, spiritual quest, or what-have-you. In fact, many students who have been admitted to the Ultras pursue gap years for a host of reasons.

I once had a student who didn't get into any of the Ultras (although she still had some in-state options), so she decided to spend a year in Spain perfecting her Spanish. She tried her luck again the next year, eventually getting into Cornell.

One of our copy editors was accepted to the University of Chicago, but she chose to take a gap year before starting college. She spent six months in China working on her language skills, and then she got an internship in Washington, D.C. with the White House Council on Environmental Quality. In her spare time, she edited the early drafts of our book (all the Oxford commas were at her behest).

Once again, if you do not get in *anywhere,* please don't lapse into a catatonic state. Try to be like Dory in *Finding Nemo*: Just keep swimming! (And look on the bright side—having short-term memory loss after you have just been shut out of the college search could be a blessing.)

Is That Your Final Answer?

Remember, three choices are made in the college process: **You decide where to apply, the colleges decide who gets in, and you decide which acceptance to take.**

So how do you make the last choice? Most college counselors recommend that you weigh the pros and cons of enrolling at each college. Key factors should include attributes of academic programs, residence halls, student life, athletics, career center, cost, climate, distance from home, and so on.

PRO TIP: College counselors will almost always tell you to go to the college where you will be the happiest. If you are weighing paying full price at a highly selective college or attending a school with a similar reputation that is offering you a scholarship, your counselor will likely tell you to take the money.

I often see students evaluate their last choice at the subatomic level. One student was fretting over an 8-to-1 student-faculty ratio versus a 9-to-1 (!). Another liberal arts student worried about attending Yale over Princeton because Princeton's engineering school was "better." (My response: *Even by your own cray-cray logic, that is nuts*). Yet another student, who was deciding between two amazing schools, looked at me and said, "I just want to go where I'll be happiest." I said that short of enrolling in one school, going through four years, building a time machine, and enrolling in the other and then comparing notes, she would never know. Lastly, there was a girl who gave a bump to one college because it had (I kid you not) more "ugly girls." She reasoned that it meant less competition.

Let's be real: High school is mostly terrible—that is why God created college. Chances are strong that you will have a fantastic experience regardless of where you go. Every year, I have students in tears in the spring because of their perceived lack of college options, yet 99 times out of a 100, those students are ecstatic in the fall.

GRADUATION DAY

CHAPTER 14

I just can't wait till my ten-year reunion
I'm gonna bust down the double doors,
And when I stand on these tables before you
You will know what all this time was for.

— *John Mayer, "No Such Thing"*

O NCE YOU GRADUATE from high school, you are not *quite* done with the college process. For instance, you still have to submit your final transcript. At the end of the day, your academic record belongs to you, not the college, so it is possible your college may contact you directly to request the transcript. Make sure everything gets done on time.

College counselors are pushed beyond sanity every year when students fail to request the final transcript or the colleges lose track of the paperwork that counselors have already submitted (see Chapter 11). Most high schools tend to shut down over the summer, which makes the task doubly difficult if a student receives a notification from the college saying that all paperwork is not in order.

When dealing with errant documents, remember the mantra of Kevin Bacon during the Homecoming parade riot in *Animal House:* "Remain calm! All is well!"

If you took all your high school classes at just one school, your chance of encountering a snafu is reduced, but if you took a class or two at a community college or from an online entity, you might have a tougher time tracking everything down. Be proactive. Once you have decided where you will go to college, get those requests in— pronto. There are dozens if not hundreds of other graduates also making similar requests, and college counselors and registrars are not at your beck and call.

Students also need to be on top of housing forms and deposits. You snooze and you might lose a spot on campus. Ditto for requesting scholarships and other funding sources.

Once you graduate from high school, you will find that your alma mater is already transitioning to help all those rising seniors. You will soon be on your own.

The Roommate Situation

So you've decided where you will go to college, but what are you going to do about a roommate?

Some colleges do not let you request a freshman roommate. If that is the case, there is nothing more for you to do except fill out the roommate questionnaire and wait to discover your roomie's identity.

PRO TIP: Many housing offices will let you pick your roommate(s). Contrary to popular belief, they want to make students happy. And if it doesn't work out, you can't blame it on the college.

As a former freshman advisor, I evaluated all freshman questionnaires with a grain of salt. Half the time the parents filled out the forms for the students without their knowledge or input, and the rest of the time the parents were looking over their child's shoulder while the forms were completed.

This failure to communicate honestly led to more than a few unfortunate roommate pairings.

Full Disclosure: As freshmen advisors, we knew that we would have the same number of successful roommate pairings as we did failures, whether we spent 100 hours poring over all the data or just 10 hours, so we tried not to overthink it too much.

If you have the option of requesting a roommate, do you really want to ask someone you know, be it a close friend or a not-so-close acquaintance, to spend that first year in close quarters? Do you want a known quantity, or will you let fate decide? Are you going to keep playing it safe, or will you cast off the last vestiges of your old life, throw caution to the wind, and start flying by the seat of your pants (whatever that means)?

If you do not know anyone going to your college, you can always check the incoming freshman Facebook page or whatever other social media platform the school uses to connect their new students. However you choose, you will find that the girls usually are a lot more conscientious about pre-selecting a roommate than the guys.

#Adulting

The summer after graduating from high school is a tricky time for students and parents alike.

First, there will be a deluge of graduation parties and events, both large and small.

There might be some post-graduation travel. Whether your family takes you to Universal Studios, you go backpacking across Europe, or you stay home and chill out all summer, enjoy the journey. You will have plenty of time in college to worry about classes, internships, and jobs.

If you are concerned about having enough discretionary money at college to last you all year, you will probably need a job to pad your bank account.

And before you head off to school, you might need to acquire some basic life skills:

Learn how to do your own laundry or else you might turn an entire load of clothes pink like I did my freshman year when I washed a bright red shirt with all my whites and my favorite baseball jersey.

Discover how much things cost in the real world before you go on a spending spree in college. Learn about credit card debt. And figure out how to tip (18 to 20 percent).

If you are bringing a car to college, and you do not have AAA, be sure you know how to jumpstart a dead battery, change a tire, and de-ice a frozen windshield.

PRO TIP: For you southerners going to school up north, do not pour hot water on a frozen car windshield or try using the windshield wipers before checking to make sure they are not frozen in place.

Separation Anxiety

When summer is over and it's time for you to head off to college, indulge your parents. Let them take all the photos they want of you and your new campus, and your dorm room, and your roommate, and your roommate's parents, and anything else their sentimental hearts may desire.

Mom and Dad, you have to leave eventually. Do not be that parent who stays the entire orientation week just in case your child needs anything. Or worse, do not be that parent who tries to stay *in* the dorm room with their son during O-week. And do not stick around for days watching your child from afar. All these incidents have actually happened in just the last few years. I even had one mom who moved all the way to New Haven, Connecticut, just so she could stay close to her daughter at Yale. Don't be that parent.

Just remember what the buffalo said when his boy went off to college: "Bison!"

Everyone deals with separation differently, and it will likely affect you in ways in which you are unprepared. I thought I had handled my older son's college move-in pretty well. By the time we drove away, it was clearly time to give him his space. A week later, as I was grocery shopping, I started getting all weepy when I realized that I didn't need to buy any Cinnamon Toast Crunch.

College Search, Part II?

If you happen to have another child at home, I hope you took good notes. Like Cutty and Slim Charles on *The Wire* pointed out:

CUTTY
The game done changed.
SLIM CHARLES
The game's the same, just got more fierce...

Of course, the competition will get tougher. The entire educational establishment has been selling that same narrative for almost 40 years, so why would they stop now?

Who knows how things will change? Maybe next year the Coalition will require that students begin creating their "lock box" in sixth grade, or the SAT will introduce a Science section, or the University of Chicago will announce absolutely free tuition for all families, regardless of income.

Wouldn't it be pretty to think so?

I Wish That I Knew What I Know Now, When I Was Younger

There are many things in life that do not live up to expectations, but college is usually not one of them. More than anything, college is an opportunity to reinvent yourself. Or discover yourself. Or both.

If you didn't like your friends in high school, try to seek out the kind of people you want to be around in college.

If you had a certain reputation in high school, then change it. Do not resign yourself to being a brain, an athlete, a basket case, a princess, or a criminal.

One excellent piece of advice I heard from a college baseball coach was to hang out with people in college who could not care less about what you're good at.

Do not talk all the time about your friends back home. Your college friends do not know them. Move on.

Do not bring up your high school grades, GPA, or SAT/ACT scores in college. You got in, be happy.

And as Monty Python sagely advised in *The Meaning of Life*: "Try to be nice to people, avoid eating fat, read a good book every now and then, get some walking in, and try and live together in peace and harmony with people of all creeds and nations."

What's in a Name?

If you are looking to transform your identity in college, there is no better way than to change your name.

In high school, I wanted everyone to call me Dave because Dave is your buddy, Dave is your pal. David is your accountant.

No one in high school ever called me Dave, no matter how hard I tried, so I gave up. But when I got to college, suddenly everyone called me Dave. It was just a fact of life that in college everyone tended to use the shortest version of a name. Every William became Bill. Russell became Russ. Katherine was Kat. Debbie became Deb. And if you were a guy from Texas going to school out of state, then you were Tex.

One guy I met during freshman orientation looked like a member of a biker gang—complete with an impressively full beard. His name was Scott, but he insisted that everyone call him Zonker. And since he looked and acted like a Zonker, no one thought anything of it. Five years later, I ran into someone from Zonker's high school, so I asked if he knew Zonker. *No.* What about Scott? *Oh yeah, I know him. Who's this Zonker fellow?*

Across campus, more freshmen were making introductions. One guy was named John. Then another guy named John joined in. Finally, another John showed up, who introduced himself like Agent 007: "I'm John, John Casey." Since there were already too many Johns, someone said, "Nice to meet you, John-John." And thus he was John-John for the next four years.

Transgender students often change their names (and pronouns) to fit their preferred identity. If your high school community or family did not fully embrace your new name (or you haven't made the switch yet), you may find college to be a more accepting place to make the transition.

If you are wise, you probably already scrubbed your online profile a bit when you started applying to colleges. For a few years, all my students changed their Facebook names to something silly or coded so colleges would not be able to see their pages (Guess what? They still could). Today high school students rarely bother with Facebook at all.

Go ahead and use Snapchat, Instagram, or Twitter to keep up with your friends and family, but eventually you will find that college has a lot to keep you busy, and you might end up losing touch, even with your BFFs. Don't worry, there is always Thanksgiving break for you all to catch up.

And when you do reconnect with your old friends, try not to play the "who is having the best college experience game" when you see each other. Some of you will have an amazing, transformative time in college, but it will not always be smooth sailing, especially that first year.

In college, you will hopefully discover what brings you joy.

You will meet some of the most amazing people ever, and as long as you are still not trying to be overly competitive with them, you might just learn from them as much as you do from your professors. Your classmates will become your friends, co-workers, bridesmaids, groomsmen, and perhaps your partner. But you have to stop playing Fortnight in your dorm room long enough to allow any of it happen.

Who knows, maybe one day you will even become an admissions tour guide who will help shape the collegiate future of some high school kid who is just as scared, excited, and eager as you once were.

If you have been on a college tour, then you know that practically every single one concludes the exact same way: the tour guide stops at the final location and tells the group about their journey to this school.

This is the final stop on our virtual tour. Wherever your college journey takes you, we hope that *Achieving Admission* has been an edifying and entertaining experience that will help you write your own story with more laughs and wonderful memories than you might have had otherwise.

Excelsior!

RESOURCES

"2019-2020 Common Application Prompts." *The Common Application.* www.commonapp.org.

"ACT Scores Down for 2016 U.S. Grad Class Due to Increased Percentage of Students Tested." *ACT*, 24 August 2016, www.act.org.

Adams, Cydney. "High school senior accepted to 149 colleges, offered over $7M in scholarships." *CBS News*, 26 May 2017. www.cbsnews.com.

Anderson, Nick. "Top colleges put thousands of applicants in wait-list limbo, and some won't admit any." *Washington Post.* 16 April 2016.

Bernhard, Meg P. "The Making of a Harvard Feeder School." *Harvard Crimson.* 13 December 2013.

Beshore, Brent. "5 Minutes Early Is On Time; On Time Is Late; Late Is Unacceptable." *Forbes.* 2 August 2015.

Breslaw, Anna. "Beware the Manic Pixie Dream Boyfriend." *New York Magazine.* 13 September 2015.

Bruni, Frank. *Where You Go Is Not Who You'll Be.* Grand Central Publishing, 2015.

Carnegie, Dale. *How to Win Friends and Influence People.* Pocket Books, 2010.

Clinedinst, Melissa, Anna-Maria Koranteng, and Tara Nicola. "State of College Admission." *NACAC*, 2015, www.nacacnet.org.

Downing, Margaret. "HISD's College Success Program Uncovered Inequities and Is Changing the Status Quo." *Houston Press*, 21 June 2016.

Espenshade, Thomas J. and Chang Y. Chung. "The Opportunity Cost of Admission Preferences at Elite Universities." *Social Science Quarterly*, vol. 86, no. 2, June 2005, pp. 293-305.

Friedersdorf, Conor. "The Typical College Student Is Not Who You Think It Is." *The Atlantic.* 1 July 2016.

Gentile, Sal and Win Rosenfeld. "Presidentially: Are colleges encouraging atheism?" *PBS*, 10 February 2012, www.pbs.org.

Gladwell, Malcolm. "Food Fight." *Revisionist History* podcast. 14 July 2016.

Hoover, Eric. "One of College Confidential's Founders Says Site 'Turned Sour'." *Chronicle of Higher Education,.* 1 May 2013, www.chronicle.com.

Jackson, Abby. "This essay got a high-school senior into 5 Ivy League schools and Stanford." *Business Insider.* 1 April 2016.

Jacobs, Peter. "Kid who got into every Ivy League school is going to the University of Alabama—and it's a brilliant decision" *Business Insider.* 14 May 2015.

Kaminer, Ariel. "Applications by the Dozen, as Anxious Seniors Hedge College Bets." *New York Times.* 15 November 2014.

Klein, Jesse. "Relative Wealth." *Michigan Daily.* 16 February 2015.

Kolodner, Meredith. "States moving college scholarship money away from the poor, to the wealthy and middle class." *The Hechinger Report.* 22 June 2015.

Konnikova, Maria. "How Facebook Makes Us Unhappy." *New Yorker.* 10 Sept. 2013.

Maeroff, Gene I. "Admissions Week Frenzy." *New York Times.* 21 April 1978.

Mellon, Ericka. "Grier alarmed about possible grade inflation at HISD." *Houston Chronicle.* 29 February 2012.

Murphy, James S. "The Undervaluing of School Counselors." *The Atlantic.* 16 September 2016.

NACAC. "State-By-State Student-to-Counselor Ratio Report." www.schoolcounselor.org

Newitz, Annalee. "An AI invented a bunch of new paint colors that are hilariously wrong." *Ars Technica,* 19 May 2017, www.arstechnica.com.

Otto, Frank. "Why a Decline in Applications is Good for Drexel." *Drexel Now.* 21 January 2015.

Quirk, Matthew. "The Best Class Money Can Buy." *The Atlantic.* November 2005.

Radish, Tiffany. "William Shatner Interview S#*! My Dad Says." Collider.com. 19 September 2010.

Rabin, Nathan. "The Bataan Death March of Whimsy Case File #1: *Elizabethtown.*" *The A.V. Club.* 25 January 2007.

Sablich, Liz. "7 findings that illustrate racial disparities in education." *Brookings.* 6 June 2016.

Scelfo, Julie. "Suicide on Campus and the Pressure of Perfection." *New York Times.* 27 July 2015.

Selingo, Jeffrey. "Despite strong economy, worrying financial signs for higher education." *Washington Post.* 3 August 2018.

Shyong, Frank. "For Asian Americans, a changing landscape on college admissions." *Los Angeles Times.* 21 February 2015.

Teitell, Beth. "Everything Counts in the College Visit." *Boston Globe.* 11 June 2015.

Webley, Kayla. "As College Applications Rise, So Does Indecision." *Time.* 1 May 2013.

Wermund, Benjamin. "Trump blamed as U.S. colleges lure fewer foreign students." *Politico.* 23 April 2018.

Winerman, Lea. "E-mails and egos." *Monitor on Psychology,* vol. 37, no. 2, February 2006, p. 16.

"You choose." *The Economist.* 16 December 2010.

Zou, Ben. "When inclusion excludes." *Daily Pennsylvanian.* 28 July 2016.

ABOUT THE AUTHORS

David H. Nathan has taught high school English and journalism in Houston for over 25 years. He has worked as an independent educational consultant specializing in helping students write college essays, including his two sons who recently completed the college admissions process. He has also compiled and edited three books of baseball quotations, most recently *The McFarland Book of Baseball Quotations* (3d ed. 2011), and has been published in numerous newspapers and magazines. He earned his B.A. from Rice University.

Nick J. Accrocco has worked as an admissions counselor at Vanderbilt University, the University of Pennsylvania, and American University. For the past 11 years, he has worked as both a high school college counselor and an online instructor at Rice University's Center for College Readiness. He earned his B.A. from Vanderbilt University, his M.Ed. in Higher Education Administration from Vanderbilt University's George Peabody College of Education & Human Development, his graduate certificate in College Counseling from the University of California-Los Angeles and his EdD in Professional Leadership from the University of Houston.

Contributors

Brooke Kushwaha is editor-in-chief of the Wesleyan Argus and a senior editor for the Wesleyan Groundhog. All illustrations are hers unless noted.

Clara Brotzen-Smith is a graphic artist who designed the book cover.

Aileen Zhang is an artist and graphic designer who is studying astrophysics at the California Institute of Technology. Her illustration ("The Talk") appears on page 73.

Ashwini Bandi is a graphic designer and biochemistry major at Rice University. Her infographic ("Education Facts") appears on page 85.

Made in the USA
Lexington, KY
10 July 2019